Kaplan Publishing are constantly finding new ways to support students looking for exam success and our online resources really do add an extra dimension to your studies.

This book comes with free MyKaplan online resources so that you can study anytime, anywhere. **This free online resource is not sold separately and is included in the price of the book.**

Having purchased this book, you have access to the following online study materials:

CONTENT		AAT	
		Text	Kit
Electronic version of the book		✓	✓
Knowledge Check tests with instant answers		✓	
Mock assessments online		✓	✓
Material updates		✓	✓

How to access your online resources

Received this book as part of your Kaplan course?
If you have a MyKaplan account, your full online resources will be added automatically, in line with the information in your course confirmation email. If you've not used MyKaplan before, you'll be sent an activation email once your resources are ready.

Bought your book from Kaplan?
We'll automatically add your online resources to your MyKaplan account. If you've not used MyKaplan before, you'll be sent an activation email.

Bought your book from elsewhere?
Go to **www.mykaplan.co.uk/add-online-resources**
Enter the ISBN number found on the title page and back cover of this book.
Add the unique pass key number contained in the scratch panel below.
You may be required to enter additional information during this process to set up or confirm your account details.

This code can only be used once for the registration of this book online. This registration and your online content will expire when the examinations covered by this book have taken place. Please allow one hour from the time you submit your book details for us to process your request.

Please scratch the film to access your unique code.

Please be aware that this code is case-sensitive and you will need to include the dashes within the passcode, but not when entering the ISBN.

TAX PROCESSES FOR BUSINESSES

STUDY TEXT

Qualifications and Credit Framework

Q2022

Finance Act 2024

For assessments from 27 January 2025 until end January 2026

This Study Text supports study for the following AAT qualifications:

AAT Level 3 Diploma in Accounting

AAT Level 3 Certificate in Bookkeeping

AAT Diploma in Accounting at SCQF Level 7

KAPLAN PUBLISHING'S STATEMENT OF PRINCIPLES

LINGUISTIC DIVERSITY, EQUALITY AND INCLUSION

We are committed to diversity, equality and inclusion and strive to deliver content that all users can relate to.

We are here to make a difference to the success of every learner.

Clarity, accessibility and ease of use for our learners are key to our approach.

We will use contemporary examples that are rich, engaging and representative of a diverse workplace.

We will include a representative mix of race and gender at the various levels of seniority within the businesses in our examples to support all our learners in aspiring to achieve their potential within their chosen careers.

Roles played by characters in our examples will demonstrate richness and diversity by the use of different names, backgrounds, ethnicity and gender, with a mix of sexuality, relationships and beliefs where these are relevant to the syllabus.

It must always be obvious who is being referred to in each stage of any example so that we do not detract from clarity and ease of use for each of our learners.

We will actively seek feedback from our learners on our approach and keep our policy under continuous review. If you would like to provide any feedback on our linguistic approach, please use this form (you will need to enter the link below into your browser).

https://forms.gle/U8oR3abiPpGRDY158

We will seek to devise simple measures that can be used by independent assessors to randomly check our success in the implementation of our Linguistic Equality, Diversity and Inclusion Policy

British Library Cataloguing-in-Publication Data

A catalogue record for this book is available from the British Library.

Published by
Kaplan Publishing UK
Unit 2, The Business Centre
Molly Millars Lane
Wokingham
Berkshire
RG41 2QZ

ISBN 978-1-83996-876-1

© Kaplan Financial Limited, 2024

Printed and bound in Great Britain

The reference material in the introduction to this textbook has been supplied by the Association of Accounting Technicians. We are grateful for their permission to include this material in full.

We are grateful to HM Revenue and Customs for the provision of tax forms, which are Crown Copyright and are reproduced here with kind permission from the Office of Public Sector Information.

Information reproduced from the VAT Guide (VAT Notice 700) is also subject to Crown Copyright.

CONTENTS

STUDY TEXT

KAPLAN PUBLISHING

INTRODUCTION

HOW TO USE THESE MATERIALS

These Kaplan Publishing learning materials have been carefully designed to make your learning experience as easy as possible and to give you the best chance of success in your AAT assessments.

They contain a number of features to help you in the study process.

The sections on the Unit Guide, the Assessment and Study Skills should be read before you commence your studies.

They are designed to familiarise you with the nature and content of the assessment and to give you tips on how best to approach your studies.

STUDY TEXT

This study text has been specially prepared for the AAT qualification introduced in February 2022.

It is written in a practical and interactive style:

- key terms and concepts are clearly defined

- all topics are illustrated with practical examples with clearly worked solutions based on sample tasks provided by the AAT in the new examining style

- frequent activities throughout the chapters ensure that what you have learnt is regularly reinforced

- 'pitfalls' and 'examination tips' help you avoid commonly made mistakes and help you focus on what is required to perform well in your assessment

- 'Test your understanding' activities are included within each chapter to apply your learning and develop your understanding.

ICONS

The study chapters include the following icons throughout.

They are designed to assist you in your studies by identifying key definitions and the points at which you can test yourself on the knowledge gained, or to direct you towards other areas of your studies (past or future) where you will encounter similar issues or skills.

 Definition

These sections explain important areas of knowledge which must be understood and reproduced in an assessment.

 Example

The illustrative examples can be used to help develop an understanding of topics before attempting the activity exercises.

 Test your understanding

These are exercises which give the opportunity to assess your understanding of all the assessment areas.

 Reference material

These boxes will direct you to the AAT reference material that you can access during your real assessment. A copy of this reference material is included as an Appendix to this document.

 Foundation activities

These are questions to help ground your knowledge and consolidate your understanding on areas you're finding tricky.

 Extension activities

These questions are for if you're feeling confident or wish to develop your higher level skills.

Quality and accuracy are of the utmost importance to us so if you spot an error in any of our products, please send an email to: mykaplanreporting@kaplan.com with full details.

Our Quality Co-ordinator will work with our technical team to verify the error and take action to ensure it is corrected in future editions.

Progression

There are two elements of progression that we can measure: first how quickly learners move through individual topics within a subject; and second how quickly they move from one course to the next. We know that there is an optimum for both, but it can vary from subject to subject and from learner to learner. However, using data and our experience of learner performance over many years, we can make some generalisations.

A fixed period of study set out at the start of a course with key milestones is important. This can be within a subject, for example 'I will finish this topic by 30 June', or for overall achievement, such as 'I want to be qualified by the end of next year'.

Your qualification is cumulative, as earlier papers provide a foundation for your subsequent studies, so do not allow there to be too big a gap between one subject and another.

We know that exams encourage techniques that lead to some degree of short term retention, the result being that you will simply forget much of what you have already learned unless it is refreshed (look up Ebbinghaus Forgetting Curve for more details on this). This makes it more difficult as you move from one subject to another: not only will you have to learn the new subject; you will also have to relearn all the underpinning knowledge as well. This is very inefficient and slows down your overall progression which makes it more likely you may not succeed at all.

In addition, delaying your studies slows your path to qualification which can have negative impacts on your career, postponing the opportunity to apply for higher level positions and therefore higher pay.

You can use the following diagram showing the whole structure of your qualification to help you keep track of your progress.

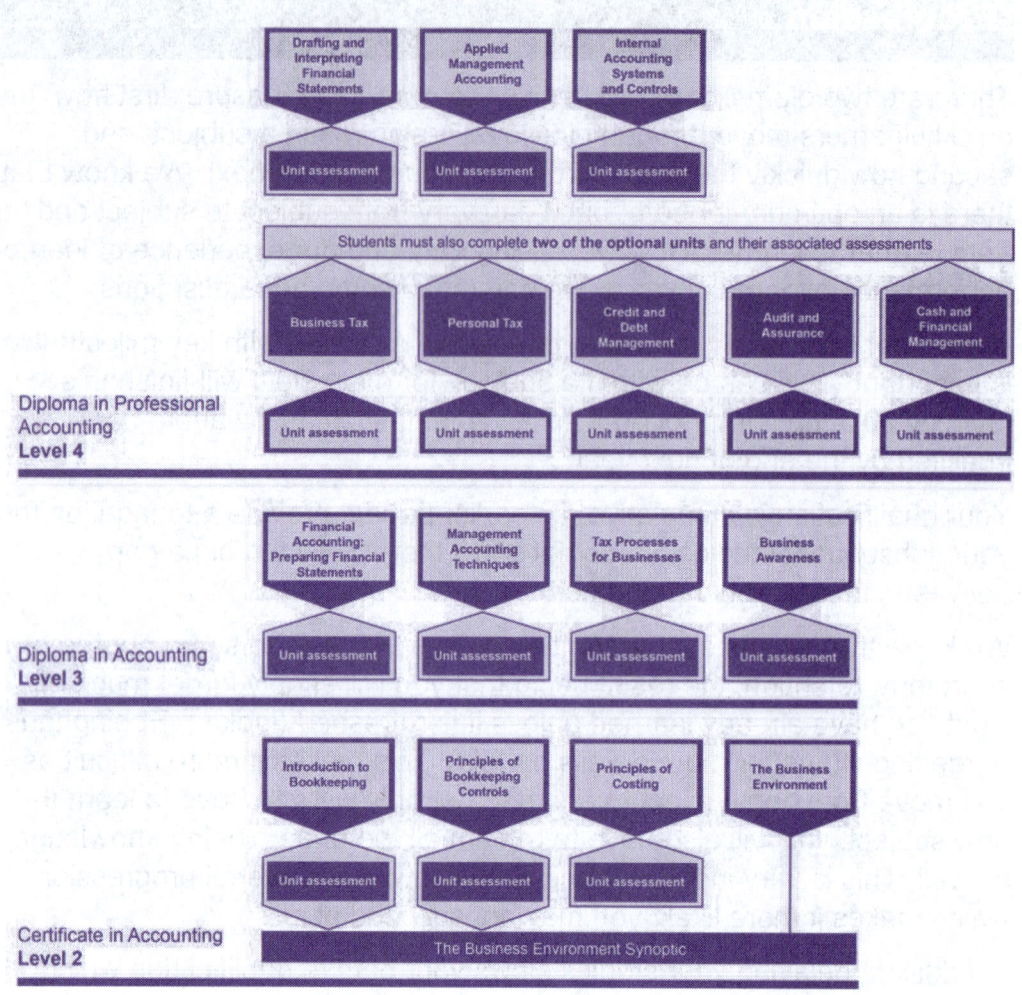

UNIT GUIDE

Introduction

This unit explores tax processes that influence the daily operations of businesses and is designed to develop learners' skills in understanding, preparing, and submitting Value Added Tax (VAT) returns to HM Revenue and Customs (HMRC). The unit provides learners with the knowledge and skills that are needed to keep businesses, employers and clients compliant with laws and practices that apply to VAT and payroll. Learners will study the relevant legislation and will appreciate the importance of maintaining their technical knowledge through monitoring updates.

For VAT, learners will understand the registration and deregistration rules, including the implications of Making Tax Digital (MTD), and the rules relating to specialist VAT schemes. Learners will be able to recognise different types of supplies and calculate VAT correctly, understanding the importance of the rules relating to the recovery of input VAT. Learners will understand the sanctions and penalties for inaccuracies, omissions and failure to make submissions and payments within the correct timescales. Learners will be able to verify the accuracy of calculations, invoices and tax points, and will learn about the correction of errors. When considering the content of the VAT return, learners will understand how to apply special rules when goods and services are imported and exported out of the UK, and how to extract the appropriate data to complete VAT returns.

In relation to payroll, learners will understand the processes for businesses involved in calculating pay and deductions. Learners will be aware of the content of documents and reports produced on software, and the timescales for submission and payment.

The application of ethical principles is threaded throughout this unit. All work must be carried out with integrity, objectivity and a high degree of professional competence. There must be due care with regards to confidentiality about any personal data being processed and, from a business protection aspect, with the correct approach to professional behaviour. Learners will understand how to communicate VAT and payroll matters to relevant individuals and organisations.

Learning outcomes

On completion of this unit, the learner will be able to:

- Understand legislation requirements relating to VAT

- Calculate VAT

- Review and verify VAT returns

- Understand the principles of payroll

- Report information within the organisation

Scope of content

To perform this unit effectively you will need to know and understand the following:

Chapter

1 Understand legislation requirements relating to VAT

1.1 UK tax law principles relating to VAT   1, 2

Learners need to understand:

- that HMRC is the relevant tax authority for VAT in the UK

- that VAT is a tax on consumer spending, charged on taxable supplies by taxable persons, including whether the tax charged falls on registered businesses or the end user

- HMRC's rights in respect of inspection of records and visits to registered businesses

- HMRC's rules about: what records should be kept, electronic invoicing, authorised accounting software, how long VAT records should be retained, electronic filing and digital tax return submission, i.e. MTD.

1.2 VAT registration and deregistration requirements   1, 2

Learners need to understand:

- the registration and deregistration thresholds for the normal VAT scheme, and how to apply them

- the definitions of, taxable supplies, standard-rated supplies, reduced-rated supplies, zero-rated supplies, exempt supplies and supplies outside the scope of VAT.

- what is meant by the historic turnover method (historic test) and the future turnover method (future test), and how to comply with them in respect of registration

- the circumstances in which voluntary registration may be beneficial to the business and for voluntary and compulsory deregistration.

		Chapter
1.3	**Filing and payment of VAT returns**	5

Learners need to understand:

- the timing and frequency of: filing VAT returns under the normal scheme and payment/re-payment of VAT under the normal scheme

- the circumstances in which monthly accounting may be beneficial to the business

- how statutory time limits for making payments differ depending on the payment method used

- that compatible software must be used and authorised for submitting VAT returns under MTD.

1.4	**Special Schemes**	5

Learners need to understand:

- the thresholds and qualification criteria for the special VAT schemes:

  - annual accounting schemes

  - cash accounting schemes

  - flat rate scheme

- the timing and frequency of: filing VAT returns, payment/re-payment of VAT

- the circumstances for voluntary and compulsory withdrawal from special schemes.

1.5	**Implications for non-compliance with VAT regulations**	7

Learners need to understand:

- the powers of HMRC to penalise a business that has failed to register for VAT

- the details of the penalty regime applicable to non-registration or late registration

- how the penalty regime applies to late submission or non-submission of VAT returns (excluding changes in filing frequency)

- the powers of assessment that HMRC has in respect of failure to submit VAT returns

Chapter

- the details of the penalty and interest regime applicable to late or non-payment of VAT due

- the consequences of failing to: correct errors properly, report an error when required to do so

- the operational and legal consequences of incorrect recovery of VAT.

2   Calculate VAT

2.1   Extracting relevant data from accounting records   1, 3, 6

Learners need to understand:

- relevant sources of VAT information needed by a business

- how to identify relevant accounting records that cover the required period of each VAT return

- how to identify and extract relevant revenue, expenditure and VAT figures from the accounting records

- how to validate data and determine that the figures extracted have come from original and verified source documents.

- the benefits of accounting software in identifying errors, e.g. incorrect VAT rate.

2.2   VAT invoices   3

Learners need to understand:

- the contents and form of a VAT invoice: simplified VAT invoices, modified VAT invoices, e-invoicing requirements, mixed-rated supplies

- how to determine the tax point of an invoice, both basic and actual, when there are: advance payments, deposits, continuous supplies, goods on sale or return

- the significance of the correct tax point for: eligibility for special VAT schemes, applying the correct rate of VAT, determining the correct VAT period

- the time limits for issuing VAT invoices: 14-day rules, 30-day rules

2.3   **VAT calculations**

Learners need to understand:

- the difference between inputs and outputs, and between input tax and output tax

- the automation of calculations through use of accounting software

- rounding rules on VAT calculation

- rules for VAT when prompt payment discounts (PPD) are offered to customers

- the different implications of exempt supplies and of zero-rated supplies, and the effect on recovery of input tax

- how partial exemption works, the de-minimis limit and how this affects the recovery of input tax

- the identification of what cannot be claimed as input VAT: expenditure on employee and business contact entertaining, including that of mixed groups; purchases and sales of cars and vans, assets with private use

- the VAT rules on fuel scale charges, how to apply them and their effect on the VAT payable or reclaimable

- how to apply bad debt relief, when this is available and what time limits apply

- how to account for postponed import VAT

- calculate VAT on: standard-rated supplies, reduced-rated supplies

- calculate VAT when given the net or the gross amount of the supply

- calculate the VAT payable/repayable for a VAT period from information such as: sales and purchases invoices, credit notes issued and received, cash and petty cash transaction receipts; deposits, advance payments and delayed payments; adjustments made for: fuel scale charges, bad debts, input VAT that cannot be claimed

- calculate the impact on VAT of: PPD, fuel scale charges, bad debts, items on which input VAT cannot be reclaimed

- calculate VAT for international trade: imports and exports.

3   Review and verify VAT returns

3.1   Make adjustments for errors & omissions in VAT returns   6, 7

Learners need to understand:

- if previous period errors or omissions can be corrected by amendments on current VAT returns

- the thresholds and deadlines where previous period errors or omissions must be declared, including the timescales during which corrections can be made

- when previous period errors or omissions must be separately reported rather than corrected on current VAT returns

- when to report given previous period errors or omissions that cannot be corrected on current VAT returns

- calculate and process the appropriate adjustments for given previous period errors

- recognise the impact that the adjustments for previous period errors will have on VAT.

3.2 **Verify information contained within VAT returns** 6, 7

Learners need to understand:

- what is included in all relevant boxes of the VAT return

- how imports and exports are treated on a VAT return

- the importance of checking the VAT return before submission

- how to identify reasons for any given differences between the VAT return and the accounting records

- review VAT returns from accounting information

- reconcile the VAT return to accounting records.

4 **Understand principles of payroll**

4.1 **Employer responsibilities of payroll** 8

Learners need to understand:

- that payroll is operated by businesses or individuals who employ staff

- that HMRC is the relevant tax authority for payroll

- HMRC's powers to require businesses to comply with: regulations about registration, record keeping, submissions of returns, payment of amounts due

- HMRC's rights in respect of inspection of records and visits.

- HMRC's rules about: what records should be kept, software, how payroll records should be retained, how long payroll records should be retained

- the difference between gross pay, taxable pay and net pay

- that businesses are required to make statutory deductions from gross pay: Pay As You Earn (PAYE), national insurance contributions (NICs), student loans, pensions

- that businesses may be required to make non-statutory deductions from gross pay

- when businesses or individuals are required to register as an employer•that employers are entitle

- the data protection principles specifically related to the personal data of employees.

Learners will be able to

- calculate the following: gross pay, taxable pay, deductions from employees' pay, net pay, the amount due to HMRC

- reconcile gross pay to net pay and/or taxable pay.

Note: learners will be provided with figures from which to calculate these values.

Exclusion: the calculation of income tax, national insurance contributions (NICs) and student loan deductions.

4.2   Operating payroll   9

Learners need to understand:

- the outline content of forms produced for payroll: payslips, P45s, P60s, P11Ds

- that employers must produce and distribute forms to employees within the required time period

- that payroll reports must be submitted to HMRC by employers in real time (RTI)

- the content of full payment submissions (FPS) and the employer payment summary (EPS) reports submitted under RTI

- that employers must report to HMRC employee payments and employee changes within the required timescale

- the statutory time limits for submitting payroll returns and making payment to HMRC

- the consequences of late filing and/or payment.

5	**Report information within the organisation**	
5.1	**Communicating information on VAT and payroll related matters**	1, 2, 3, 5, 6, 9

Learners need to understand:

- who to report relevant information to

- when a query is beyond current experience or expertise and so should be referred to a line manager

- the significant effect on cash flows and cash budgeting of the requirements to make payments on time to HMRC

Learners need to be able to:

- communicate the appropriate time limits for submitting returns and making payments to appropriate persons.

- communicate the effects of new legislation to the appropriate person

- provide appropriate information for VAT: the completion of the VAT return, the discovery of current and previous period errors and omissions, determining whether to correct or disclose errors and omissions; penalties and assessments; the effects of a change in VAT rate or other regulatory changes, the effect on VAT of a change in business operations, effects of adopting special VAT schemes on payment or recovery of VAT

- provide appropriate information for payroll: the completion of payroll reports, penalties, the effects of regulatory changes.

5.2 **Legislation, regulation, guidance and codes of practice**   1, 6, 9

Learners need to understand:

- where to find information regarding changes to VAT and payroll law and practice

- the importance of seeking authorisation before returns are submitted

- the relevance of data protection, information security and confidentiality to VAT and payroll practice

- the importance of maintaining up to date and relevant knowledge

- the importance of ethical behaviour in relation to VAT and payroll

- the importance of updating any accounting software regarding changes to VAT and payroll legislation

- the importance of acting in good faith and exercising care in relation to facts or information presented on behalf of clients or employers when dealing with HMRC, according to the AAT Code of Professional Ethics.

Delivering this unit

This unit links with the following units:

- Level 3 Business Awareness

- Level 3 Financial Accounting: Preparing Financial Statements

- Level 3 Management Accounting Techniques.

THE ASSESSMENT

Test specification for this unit assessment

Assessment type	Marking type	Duration of exam
Computer based assessment	Computer marked	1 hour 30 minutes

The assessment for this unit consists of 8 compulsory tasks.

The competency level for AAT assessment is 70%.

Learning outcomes		Weighting
1	Understand legislation requirements relating to VAT	25%
2	Calculate VAT	30%
3	Review and verify VAT returns	20%
4	Understand principles of payroll	15%
5	Report information within the organisation	10%
Total		100%

AAT reference material

Reference material is provided in this assessment. During your assessment, you will be able to access reference material through a series of clickable links on the right of every task. These will produce pop-up windows, which can be moved or closed.

The AAT reference material is available to study before the assessment, via the AAT website, and in the appendix to this study text.

APPRENTICESHIP LEARNERS ONLY

UNIT LINK TO THE END POINT ASSESSMENT (EPA)

To achieve the Assistant Accountant apprenticeship leaners must pass all of the assessments in the Diploma in Accounting, complete a portfolio and reflective discussion and complete a synoptic/knowledge assessment.

The synoptic/knowledge assessment is attempted following completion of the individual AAT units and it draws upon knowledge and understanding from those units. It will be appropriate for learners to retain their study materials for individual units until they have successfully completed the synoptic assessment for that apprenticeship level.

With specific reference to this unit, the following learning objectives are also relevant to the knowledge assessment:

LO1   Understand legislation requirements relating to VAT.

LO2   Calculate VAT.

LO3   Review and verify VAT returns.

LO4   Understand principles of payroll.

KAPLAN PUBLISHING

STUDY SKILLS

Preparing to study

Devise a study plan

Determine which times of the week you will study.

Split these times into sessions of at least one hour for study of new material. Any shorter periods could be used for revision or practice.

Put the times you plan to study onto a study plan for the weeks from now until the assessment and set yourself targets for each period of study – in your sessions make sure you cover the whole course and the associated test your understanding questions.

If you are studying more than one unit at a time, try to vary your subjects as this can help to keep you interested and see subjects as part of wider knowledge.

When working through your course, compare your progress with your plan and, if necessary, re-plan your work (perhaps including extra sessions) or, if you are ahead, do some extra revision/practice questions.

Effective studying

Active reading

You are not expected to learn the text by rote, rather, you must understand what you are reading and be able to use it to pass the assessment and develop good practice.

A good technique is to use SQ3Rs – Survey, Question, Read, Recall, Review:

1   Survey the chapter

Look at the headings and read the introduction, knowledge, skills and content, so as to get an overview of what the chapter deals with.

2   Question

Whilst undertaking the survey ask yourself the questions you hope the chapter will answer for you.

3   Read

Read through the chapter thoroughly working through the Test Your Understanding (TYU) questions and, at the end, making sure that you can meet the learning objectives highlighted on the first page.

4   Recall

At the end of each section and at the end of the chapter, try to recall the main ideas of the section/chapter without referring to the text. This is best done after short break of a couple of minutes after the reading stage.

5   Review

Check that your recall notes are correct.

You may also find it helpful to re-read the chapter to try and see the topic(s) it deals with as a whole.

Note taking

Taking notes is a useful way of learning, but do not simply copy out the text.

The notes must:

- be in your own words

- be concise

- cover the key points

- be well organised

- be modified as you study further chapters in this text or in related ones.

Trying to summarise a chapter without referring to the text can be a useful way of determining which areas you know and which you don't.

Three ways of taking notes

1   Summarise the key points of a chapter

2   Make linear notes

A list of headings, subdivided with sub-headings listing the key points.

If you use linear notes, you can use different colours to highlight key points and keep topic areas together.

Use plenty of space to make your notes easy to use.

3   Try a diagrammatic form

The most common of which is a mind map.

To make a mind map, put the main heading in the centre of the paper and put a circle around it.

Draw lines radiating from this to the main sub-headings, which again have circles around them.

Continue the process from the sub-headings to sub-sub-headings.

Annotating the text

You may find it useful to underline or highlight key points in your study text – but do be selective.

You may also wish to make notes in the margins.

Revision phase

Kaplan has produced material specifically designed for your final examination preparation for this unit.

These include pocket revision notes and an exam kit that includes a bank of revision questions specifically in the style of the syllabus.

Further guidance on how to approach the final stage of your studies is given in these materials.

Further reading

In addition to this text, you should also read the "Accounting Technician" magazine every month to keep abreast of any guidance from the AAT and chief assessors.

REFERENCE MATERIAL

AAT reference material

Reference material is provided in this assessment. During your assessment you will be able to access reference material through a series of clickable links on the right of every task. These will produce pop-up windows which can be moved or closed.

The reference material has been included in this study text (below). This is based on the version of the reference material that was available at the time of going to print.

The full version of the reference material is available for download from the AAT website.

Level 3 Tax Processes for Businesses (TPFB)
reference material

Finance Act 2024 – for assessments from 27 January 2025

aat.org.uk

Reference material for AAT assessment of Tax Processes for Businesses

Introduction

This document comprises data that you may need to consult during your Tax Processes for Businesses computer-based assessment.

The material can be consulted during the practice and live assessments by using the reference materials section at each task position. It's made available here so you can familiarise yourself with the content before the assessment.

Do not take a print of this document into the exam room with you*.

This document may be changed to reflect periodical updates in the computer-based assessment, so please check you have the most recent version while studying. This version is based on **Finance Act 2024** and is for use in **AAT Q2022 assessments in 2025**.

*Unless you need a printed version as part of reasonable adjustments for particular needs, in which case you must discuss this with your tutor at least six weeks before the assessment date.

Contents

1. Rates of VAT

Taxable supplies:

Standard rate	20%
Reduced rate	5%
Zero rate	0%

Non-taxable supplies have no VAT applied:

- Exempt
- Outside the scope of VAT

2. Registration and deregistration for VAT

Registration threshold	£90,000
Deregistration threshold	£88,000

Compulsory registration	Notify HMRC	Registration effective from
Historic test	Within 30 days of the end of the month threshold was exceeded	First day of the second month after threshold exceeded
Future test	Before the end of the 30 day period	From the start of the 30 day period

Deregistration	Notify HMRC	Deregistration effective from
Compulsory	Within 30 days of the business ceasing to make taxable supplies	Date of cessation
Voluntary	Evidence that taxable supplies will not exceed the VAT deregistration threshold in the next 12 months	Date request received by HMRC, or Agreed later date

3. Failure to register for VAT

- This can result in a penalty for failure to notify. The penalty is a % of potential lost revenue (PLR).

Type of behaviour	Within 12 months of tax being due		12 months or more after tax was due	
	unprompted	prompted	unprompted	prompted
Non-deliberate	0-30%	10-30%	10-30%	20-30%
Deliberate but not concealed	20-70%	35-70%	20-70%	35-70%
Deliberate and concealed	30-100%	50-100%	30-100%	50-100%

- Penalties will not be applied if there is a reasonable excuse.

- HMRC will treat the business as though it had registered on time and will expect VAT to be accounted for as if it had been charged. The business has two choices:

    i. treat the invoices as VAT inclusive and absorb the VAT which should have been charged, or

    ii. account for VAT as an addition to the charges already invoiced and attempt to recover this VAT from its customers.

4. Changes to the VAT registration

HMRC must be notified of a change of:

Name, trading name or address	Within 30 days
Partnership members	Within 30 days
Agent's details	Within 30 days
Bank account details	14 days in advance
Change in business activity	Within 30 days

5. Keeping business and VAT records

Record retention period	6 years
Penalty for failure to keep records	£500

6. Contents of a VAT invoice

Full VAT invoice

- a sequential number based on one or more series which uniquely identifies the document
- the time of the supply (tax point)
- the date of issue of the document (where different to the time of supply)
- supplier's name, address, and VAT registration number
- customer's name and address
- a description sufficient to identify the goods or services supplied
- for each description, the quantity of the goods or the extent of the services, the rate of VAT, and the amount payable excluding VAT — this can be expressed in any currency
- the gross total amount payable, excluding VAT — this can be expressed in any currency
- the rate of any cash discount offered
- the total amount of VAT chargeable — this must be expressed in sterling
- the unit price (applicable to countable elements).

Simplified VAT invoices (<£250)

- suppliers name, address, and VAT registration number
- the time of supply (tax point)
- a description which identifies the goods or services supplied
- for each applicable VAT rate, the total amount payable, including VAT and the VAT rate.

Modified VAT invoices

- a full VAT invoice showing the VAT inclusive rather than VAT exclusive values.

7. Partial exemption for VAT

De minimis amount	£625 per month
Proportion of total input VAT	<50%

- Generally, a partially exempt business cannot reclaim the input tax paid on purchases that relate to exempt supplies.

- If the amount of input tax incurred relating to exempt supplies is below a minimum de minimis amount, input tax can be reclaimed in full.

- If the amount of input tax incurred relating to exempt supplies is above the de minimis amount, only the part of the input tax that related to non-exempt supplies can be reclaimed.

8. International trade and VAT

Export of goods	Zero-rated
Import of goods	UK VAT applied using postponed accounting.
Export of services	Apply UK VAT if place of supply is in the UK: • for supplies to business, place of supply is the location of the customer (outside the scope of UK VAT) • for supplies to non-business customers, place of supply is the location of the supplier (charge UK VAT).
Import of services	Reverse charge applies

9. Tax points for VAT

Basic tax point date	Date of despatch of the goods/carrying out of the service
Actual tax point date may be earlier	If either: • payment is received earlier • invoice is issued earlier. Actual tax point becomes the earlier of these two dates.
Actual tax point date may be later	If: • invoice is issued within 14 days of despatch/service (and advance payment didn't apply).

- Deposits are treated separately to final payment and so may have a different tax point.
- The tax point is always the date of payment if cash basis is being applied.
- Where services are being supplied on a continuous basis over a period in excess of a month but invoices are being issued regularly throughout the period, a tax point is created every time an invoice is issued or a payment is made, whichever happens first.
- Goods on sale or return will have a tax point date either on adoption (the customer indicates they will keep the goods) or 12 months after removal of the goods where this is earlier.

10. Time limits for issuing a VAT invoice

Within 30 days of tax point which is either:

- within 30 days of date of supply or
- within 30 days of payment if payment was in advance.

11. Blocked expenses and VAT

Input VAT cannot be recovered on blocked expenses.

Business entertainment

- The exception is that input tax can be reclaimed in respect of entertaining overseas customers, but not UK or Isle of Man customers.

- When the entertainment is in respect of a mixed group of both employees and non-employees (e.g. customers and/or suppliers), the business can only reclaim VAT on the proportion of the expenses that is for employees and on the proportion for overseas customers.

Cars

- Input VAT can only be recovered on cars if it is wholly for business (no private use).

- 50% of input VAT can be recovered when cars are hired/leased.

- VAT can be recovered on commercial vehicles such as vans/lorries.

Assets with private use

- The VAT recovery should be based only on the proportion related to business use.

12. Fuel scale charge and VAT

If the business pays for road fuel, it can deal with the VAT charged on the fuel in one of four ways:

- reclaim all of the VAT. All of the fuel must be used only for business purposes

- reclaim all of the VAT and pay the appropriate fuel scale charge (as follows) - this is a way of accounting for output tax on fuel that the business buys but that is then used for private motoring

- reclaim only the VAT that relates to fuel used for business mileage. Detailed records of business and private mileage must be kept

- do not reclaim any VAT. This can be a useful option if mileage is low and also if fuel is used for both business and private motoring. If the business chooses this option, it must apply it to all vehicles, including commercial vehicles.

The fuel scale charge is as follows:

Description of vehicle: vehicle's CO2 emissions figure	VAT inclusive consideration for a 12 month prescribed accounting period (£)	VAT inclusive consideration for a 3 month prescribed accounting period (£)	VAT inclusive consideration for a 1 month prescribed accounting period (£)
120 or less	702	174	58
125	1,050	263	87
130	1,123	279	92
135	1,191	297	98
140	1,263	315	105
145	1,331	332	110
150	1,404	350	116
155	1,471	368	122
160	1,544	385	127
165	1,612	403	134
170	1,685	420	139
175	1,752	437	145
180	1,825	455	151
185	1,893	473	157
190	1,965	490	163
195	2,033	508	169
200	2,106	526	174

Description of vehicle: vehicle's CO_2 emissions figure	VAT inclusive consideration for a 12 month prescribed accounting period (£)	VAT inclusive consideration for a 3 month prescribed accounting period (£)	VAT inclusive consideration for a 1 month prescribed accounting period (£)
205	2,174	544	180
210	2,246	560	186
215	2,314	578	192
220	2,387	596	198
225 or more	2,454	613	203

- Where the CO_2 emission figure is not a multiple of 5, the figure is rounded down to the next multiple of 5 to determine the level of the charge.

13.   Bad debt and VAT

VAT that has been paid to HMRC and which has not been received from the customer can be reclaimed as bad debt relief. The conditions are that:

    i.   the debt is more than six months and less than four years and six months old

    ii.   the debt has been written off in the VAT account and transferred to a separate bad debt account

    iii.   the debt has not been sold or handed to a factoring company

    iv.   the business did not charge more than the normal selling price for the items.

Bad debt relief does not apply when the cash accounting scheme is used because the VAT is not paid to HMRC until after the customer has paid it to the supplier.

14. Due dates for submitting the VAT return and paying electronically

Deadline for submitting return and paying VAT – quarterly accounting	1 month and 7 days after the end of the VAT period
Deadline if being paid by direct debit	HMRC will collect 3 working days after the submission deadline.

- Please see alternative submission and payment deadlines for special accounting schemes.

15. Special accounting schemes for VAT

15.1 Annual accounting scheme for VAT

Joining the scheme	Maximum (estimated) taxable turnover in the next 12 months	£1.35m
Leaving the scheme	Compulsory if taxable turnover at the end of the VAT accounting year exceeds the threshold	£1.6m
VAT returns	One annual return	2 months after the end of the accounting period
VAT payments (monthly)	Nine monthly interim payments (10% of estimated VAT bill based on previous returns)	At the end of months 4 to 12 in the accounting period
	Balancing payment	2 months after the end of the accounting period
VAT payments (quarterly)	Three interim payments (25% of estimated VAT bill based on previous returns)	At the end of months 4, 7 and 10 in the accounting period
	Balancing payment	2 months after the end of the accounting period

15.2 Cash accounting scheme for VAT

Joining the scheme	Maximum (estimated) taxable turnover in the next 12 months	£1.35m
Leaving the scheme	Compulsory if taxable turnover at the end of the VAT accounting year exceeds the threshold	£1.6m
Deadlines for submission and payment		Same as normal scheme

15.3 Flat rate scheme for VAT

Joining the scheme	Maximum taxable turnover (excluding VAT) in the next 12 months	£150,000
Leaving the scheme	On the anniversary of joining, maximum turnover in the last 12 months (including VAT) or expected turnover in next 12 months	£230,000
Discount	In first year of being VAT-registered	1%
Limited cost business	Goods cost less than either: • 2% of turnover, or • £1,000 a year	16.5%
Capital expenditure	Input tax can be recovered on individual large capital purchases	£2,000
Deadlines for submission and payment		Same as normal scheme

• The appropriate flat rate % will be provided in the assessment.

16. Errors in previous VAT returns

Adjustments can be made to correct net errors that are:

- below the reporting threshold
- not deliberate
- for an accounting period that ended less than 4 years ago.

The reporting threshold is;

- £10,000 or less or
- for net errors between £10,000 and £50,000, up to 1% of the Box 6 figure (total value of sales and all other outputs excluding any VAT) for the period in which the error was discovered

When the next VAT return is submitted, the net value of errors is added to VAT due on sales and other outputs for tax due to HMRC, or to VAT reclaimed in the period on purchases and other inputs for tax due to the business.

If the value of the net VAT error discovered is above the reporting threshold, it must be declared to HMRC separately, in writing.

17. Late submission and late payment of VAT

17.1 Late submission

Submission frequency	Penalty point threshold	Period of compliance
Annual	2 points	24 months
Quarterly	4 points	12 months

Initial penalty	£200
Subsequent penalty	£200

Removal of penalty points

Business has not reached penalty threshold	When penalty points expire depends on the date the VAT return was due. If the deadline for the VAT return was: • not the last day of a month — a penalty point expires on the last day of the month, 24 months after this • the last day of a month — a penalty point expires on the last day of the month, 25 months after this
Business has reached penalty threshold	All points will be reset to zero if both conditions below are met: • a period of compliance (meeting all submission obligations on time for the period of compliance), and • all submissions due in the preceding 24 months have been made (whether or not they were on time).

17.2 Late payment

Number of days overdue	**First late payment penalty**	**Second late payment penalty**
up to 15	None	None
16 to 30	2% on the VAT outstanding at day 15	None
31 or more	2% on the VAT outstanding at day 15 AND 2% on the VAT outstanding at day 30	A daily rate based on 4% per annum charged every day from day 31 until paid in full

17.3 Interest charged

Interest is calculated at the Bank of England base rate plus 2.5%.

The Bank of England base rate will be given in the assessment.

18. Assessment of VAT

If a VAT Return is not submitted on time, HMRC will issue a 'VAT notice of assessment of tax' which will state how much HMRC think is owed.

If HMRC issue an assessment that is too low, a penalty of up to 30% can be charged for not telling them it is incorrect within 30 days.

19. Penalties for inaccuracies in VAT return

A penalty can be charged as a percentage of the potential lost revenue (PLR):

Type of behaviour	Unprompted disclosure %	Prompted disclosure %
Careless	0 - 30	15 - 30
Deliberate	20 - 70	35 - 70
Deliberate and concealed	30 - 100	50 - 100

20. Payroll record retention

Retention period	3 years from end of tax year
Penalty for failure to maintain records	£3,000

21. Types of payroll submission

Full Payment Submission (FPS)

- File on or before employees pay day.
- Include payments to and deductions for all employees.

Employer Payment Summary (EPS)

- File if no employees were paid in the month.
- Send by the 19th of the following tax month.

22. Payroll deadlines

Registering for PAYE	You must register before the first payday. You cannot register more than 2 months before you start paying people
Month end date for PAYE	5th of each month
Payment date for monthly payroll	22nd of the following month if paid electronically. 19th otherwise. If monthly amounts are <£1,500, quarterly payments can be made
Provide employees with P60	31st May following the end of the tax year
Filing deadline for Expenses & Benefits forms	6th July following the end of the tax year
Class 1A NIC payment date	22nd July following the end of the tax year, if paying electronically. 19th July following the end of the tax year, otherwise.

23. Penalties for late submission of payroll filings

Penalties may apply if:
- the FPS was late
- the expected amount of FPSs was not filed
- an EPS was not filed.

Number of employees	Monthly penalty
1 to 9	£100
10 to 49	£200
50 to 249	£300
250 or more	£400

Penalties may not apply if:

- the FPS is late but all reported payments on the FPS are within three days of the employees' payday (unless there is regular lateness)
- a new employer is late but sends the first FPS within 30 days of paying an employee
- it is a business's first failure in the tax year to send a report on time.

24. Penalties for late payroll payment

Late payment of monthly/quarterly payments
- The first failure to pay in a tax year does not count as a default.
- Late payment penalties apply to late payments and payments of less than is due.

Number of defaults in a tax year	Penalty percentage applied to the amount that is late in the relevant tax month
1 to 3	1%
4 to 6	2%
7 to 9	3%
10 or more	4%

Additional penalties will apply if:

A monthly or quarterly amount remains outstanding after 6 months	5% of unpaid tax
A monthly or quarterly amount remains outstanding after 12 months	A further 5% of unpaid tax

These additional penalties apply even where only one payment in the tax year is late.

Late payments of amounts due annually or occasionally

30 days late	5%
6 months late	Additional 5%
12 months late	Additional 5%

25. Penalties for inaccuracies in payroll filings

A penalty can be charged as a percentage of the potential lost revenue (PLR):

Type of behaviour	Unprompted disclosure %	Prompted disclosure %
Careless	0 - 30	15 - 30
Deliberate	20 - 70	35 - 70
Deliberate and concealed	30 - 100	50 - 100

Introduction to VAT

1

Introduction

This chapter introduces some of the basic ideas of value added tax (VAT), including who it is charged to and how it is collected. One key concept to cover is that of tax points. The rules for determining the tax point are important. The tax point is the date that determines in which VAT period the VAT on transactions should be included.

This unit requires you to have knowledge of VAT rules, to be able to identify errors in VAT returns, to understand VAT penalties, and understand the powers that HMRC has.

ASSESSMENT CRITERIA

Understand UK tax law principles relating to VAT (1.1)

VAT registration and deregistration requirements (1.2)

Extracting relevant data from accounting records (2.1)

VAT calculations (2.3)

Legislation, regulation, guidance and codes of practice (5.2)

CONTENTS

1   Introduction
2   Types of supply
3   Tax point
4   HM Revenue and Customs

1 Introduction

1.1   Sources of tax law and practice

The basic rules of the UK tax system are built on several key pillars.

Firstly, tax strategies, such as the rate of VAT, are determined by the government, which is elected by the UK public through a democratic process. These strategies outline how taxes should be applied and collected.

Secondly, tax legislation forms the legal framework that governs taxation. Compliance with these laws is mandatory. Each year, the annual Finance Act updates tax legislation, ensuring it stays current and relevant.

Additionally, case law plays a crucial role in the UK tax system. This refers to the decisions made in tax-related court cases. Often, these cases involve debates over the interpretation of tax laws. The rulings from these cases are binding and provide valuable guidance on how tax laws should be understood and applied.

This helps create consistency and clarity in the application of tax laws.

1.2   What is VAT?

VAT is:

- an indirect tax on consumer spending

- charged on most goods and services supplied within the UK

- suffered by the final consumer, and

- collected by businesses on behalf of HM Revenue and Customs (HMRC).

Overview of how VAT works

VAT is collected by businesses at each stage in the production and distribution process of supplying goods and services as follows:

- businesses account to HMRC for the tax (known as output VAT) on sales

- if the customer is VAT registered and uses the goods or services for business purposes, then the customer can recover the tax which was paid over on the purchase of the item or service (known as input VAT)

- accordingly, businesses actually account to HMRC for the tax on the 'value added' to the product at that stage of the process.

Businesses are merely acting as collectors of VAT on behalf of HMRC and they do not suffer any tax.

It is only the final consumer, who cannot recover the input VAT, who suffers the tax.

VAT is therefore an indirect tax:

- because it is paid indirectly to traders when you buy most goods and services, rather than being collected directly by HMRC from the taxpayer as a proportion of their income or gains.

How VAT works is shown in the illustration below.

Assume that the rate of VAT throughout is 20%.

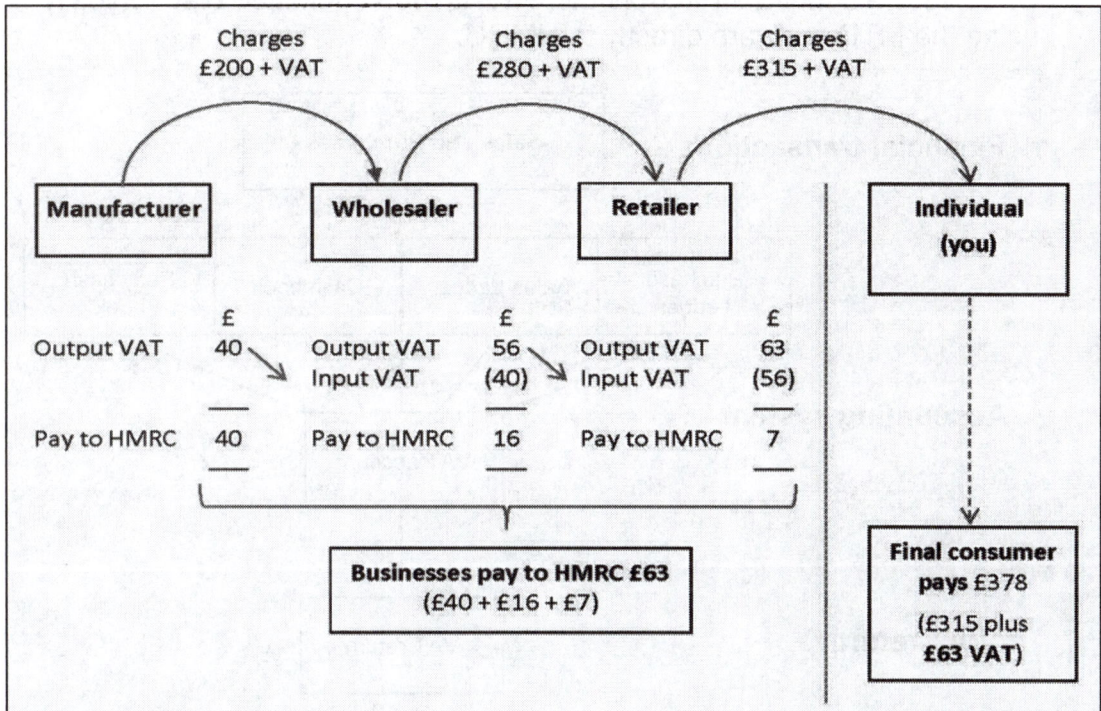

Who charges VAT?

VAT is only charged

- by **taxable persons**
- when they make **taxable supplies**
- in the **course of their business**.

VAT is not generally charged on non-business transactions.

For example, you would not have to charge VAT if you simply sold some of your spare clothes to a friend.

How is VAT recorded in the accounting system?

VAT is charged on most goods and services and the amount of VAT is shown on the sales and purchase invoices.

The VAT on invoices and credit notes is then recorded in the relevant book of prime entry, the totals from the daybooks are transferred into the general (or nominal) ledger.

The relevant ledger account for the VAT entries is the VAT control account, sometimes this is simply referred to as the VAT account.

Making Tax Digital (MTD) software then extracts the information from the VAT account and automatically completes the VAT return (Chapter 6). The business then reviews the draft return to check that the figures are correct. Once satisfied that the return is correct it is then submitted electronically using the MTD software directly to HMRC.

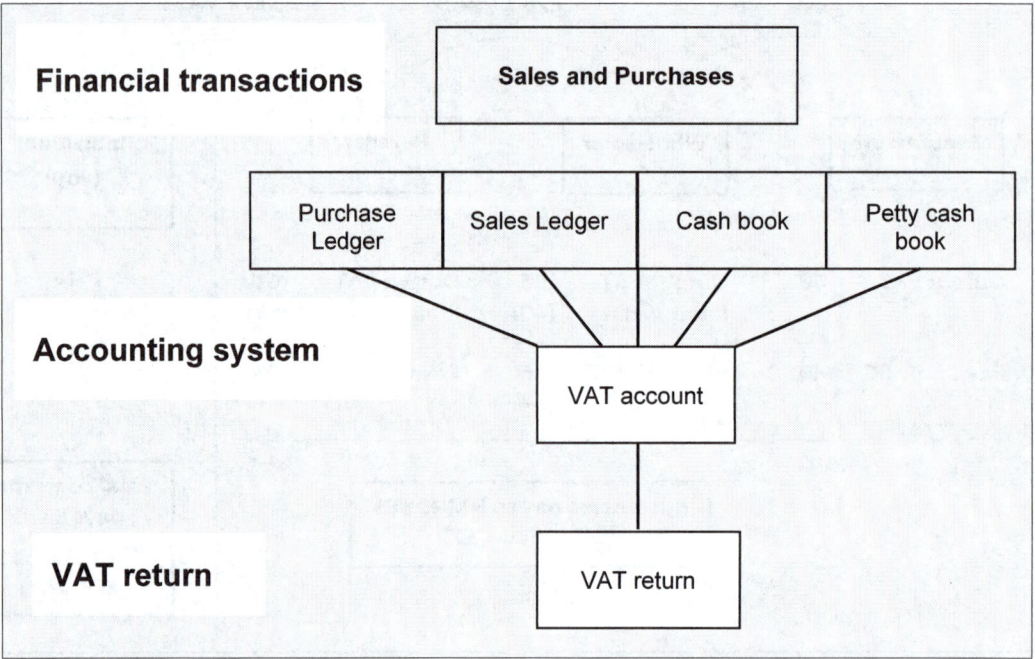

1.3 Taxable persons

 Definition

Taxable persons are businesses which are (or should be) registered for VAT.

A person can be an individual or a legal person such as a company.

VAT registration rules are dealt with in Chapter 2.

1.4 Taxable supplies

Taxable supplies (outputs) are mainly sales made by a taxable person.

Taxable supplies can also include gifts, and goods taken from the business for personal use.

1.5 Output tax

 Definition

The VAT charged on sales or taxable supplies is called **output tax**.

Taxable persons charge output tax to their customers and periodically, (usually quarterly), they pay this VAT to HMRC.

1.6 Input tax

When a business purchase goods from or pay expenses to a VAT registered supplier (inputs), it also pays VAT on those transactions.

 Definition

VAT paid by a business on purchases or expenses is called **input tax**.

VAT registered businesses are allowed to reclaim their input tax.

They do this by deducting the input tax they have paid from the output tax that they owe, and paying HMRC the net amount only.

If the input tax exceeds the output tax, then the balance is recoverable from HMRC.

 Example

A VAT registered business makes sales of £10,000 plus £2,000 of VAT. Its expenditure on purchases and expenses totals £7,000 plus £1,400 of VAT.

How much VAT is payable to HMRC?

Solution

	£
Output VAT	2,000.00
Less: Input VAT	(1,400.00)
VAT due	600.00

This means that registered businesses do not suffer VAT themselves. It is the end consumer of the goods (e.g. a member of the public like you) who suffers the VAT, as the consumer cannot recover the VAT charged.

 Test your understanding 1

Which of the following is the correct definition of a taxable person?

A   A business that is registered for VAT.

B   A business that should be registered for VAT.

C   A business that is, or should be, registered for VAT.

D   A business that makes standard-rated supplies.

 Test your understanding 2

Indicate whether the following statements are true or false.

Tick one box on each line.

		True	False
1	VAT is a direct tax.		
2	Jake is an AAT student working for a small accountancy practice. He advertises his bicycle for sale on the work notice board and sells it to one of his workmates for £100. He should not charge VAT on the sale.		
3	Businesses may keep all the VAT they collect from customers.		
4	Fred runs a small plumbing business, which is registered for VAT. He replaces a tap for a customer and charges them £60 including VAT of £10. Fred is allowed to retain the VAT charge of £10.		

KAPLAN PUBLISHING

2 Types of supply

2.1 Classification of supplies

Supplies can be **taxable**, **exempt** or **outside the scope** of VAT.

VAT is charged on taxable supplies but **not on exempt supplies** or supplies **outside the scope of VAT**. It is therefore important to be able to classify supplies correctly in order to determine whether VAT should be charged.

 Definition

Exempt supplies are supplies that the law states should not have VAT charged on them, such as insurance.

 Definition

Supplies **outside the scope of VAT** means that VAT doesn't apply to them, such as wages and dividends. They are ignored for VAT purposes. No VAT is charged and no VAT is able to be reclaimed.

Specific knowledge of which supplies are exempt will not be tested in your assessment.

2.2 Taxable supplies – rates of VAT

Taxable supplies are charged to VAT at one of three rates:

- **Zero rate**: This is a tax rate of 0%.

  It is classed as a taxable supply but is taxable at a rate of 0% i.e. the amount of VAT is zero. As it is taxable, it is considered in deciding whether a trader should register for VAT and whether input VAT is recoverable.

  An example of a zero-rated supply is children's clothing.

- **Reduced rate**: This is currently a tax rate of 5%.

  Some supplies, mainly for certain domestic and charitable purposes, are charged at the reduced rate.

  An example of reduced-rated supply is domestic fuel or power.

- **Standard rate**: This is currently a tax rate of 20%.

  Any taxable supply that is not charged at the zero or reduced rates is charged at the standard rate.

In order to calculate the amount of VAT on a **VAT-exclusive** supply that is taxable at the standard rate, you multiply by 20%.

If taxable at the reduced rate, you multiply by 5%.

In order to calculate the amount of VAT on a **VAT-inclusive** supply that is taxable at the standard rate, you multiply by 20/120. This is sometimes simplified to 1/6.

If the VAT-inclusive supply is taxable at the reduced rate, then you multiply by 5/105. This is sometimes simplified to 1/21.

These rates are summarised in the following table:

Rate of VAT	% to apply to VAT-exclusive amounts to calculate VAT	Fraction to apply to VAT-inclusive amounts to calculate VAT
Standard	20%	20/120 or 1/6
Reduced	5%	5/105 or 1/21

 Example

A business makes the following taxable supplies/ sales.

What is the output VAT in each case?

State your answer rounded down to the nearest penny.

(i)   a standard-rated supply which is £12,000 net of VAT
      (£12,000 × 20%) = £2,400.00

(ii) £12,000 inclusive of the standard rate of VAT
      (£12,000 × 20/120) = £2,000.00

(iii) £15,479 net of reduced rate VAT
      (£15,479 × 5%) = £773.95

(iv) £12,320 inclusive of reduced rate VAT
      (£12,320 × 5/105) = £586.67

Test your understanding 3

Calculate the amount of VAT in respect of the following amounts.

Item	Rate of VAT	VAT-inclusive amount	VAT-exclusive amount	VAT
		£	£	£
1	20%	472.50		
2	20%		5,250.00	
3	5%		4,230.00	
4	5%	4,284.00		

2.3 Effect of making taxable supplies

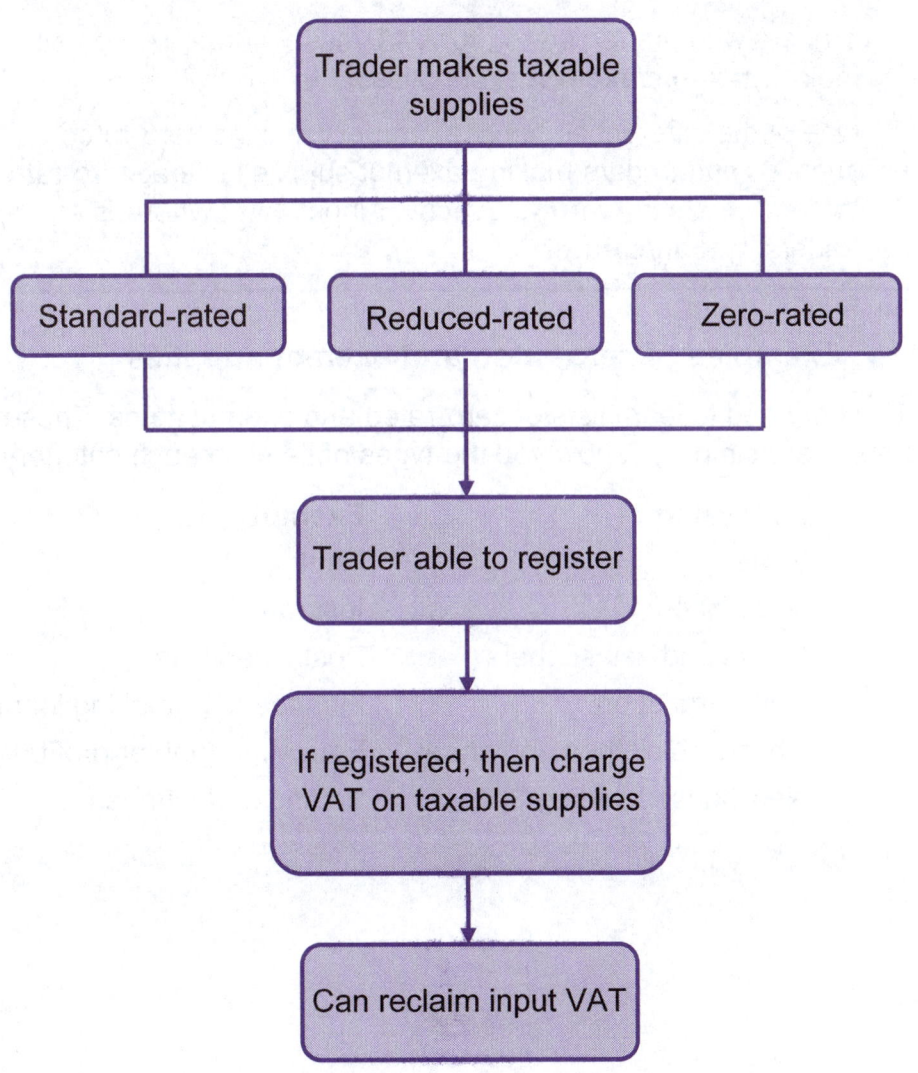

2.4 Differences between zero-rated and exempt supplies

You must be careful to distinguish between traders making zero-rated supplies and those making exempt supplies.

	Zero-rated	Exempt
Can register for VAT?	Yes	No
Charge output VAT to customers?	Yes at 0%	No
Can recover input tax?	Yes	No

 Test your understanding 4

Select which of the words in bold complete each of the following sentences correctly.

1   Traders making only exempt supplies …**can/must/cannot**…… register for VAT.

2   Traders who are registered for VAT must charge VAT on all of their ….**taxable/exempt**… supplies.

3   One of the differences between traders making zero-rated supplies and traders making exempt supplies is that zero-rated traders …….**can/cannot**… recover input VAT, whereas exempt traders …..**can/cannot**.

2.5 Examples of zero-rated and exempt supplies

You do not need to learn lists of zero-rated and exempt items. These examples are simply to show you the types of items in each category.

Zero-rated	Exempt
Water	Rent
Most food	Insurance
Books and newspapers	Postal services
Public transport	Finance (e.g. making loans)
Children's clothes and shoes	Education (not for profit)
New house building	Betting and lotteries

Test your understanding 5

Indicate whether the following statements are true or false.
Tick one box on each line.

		True	False
1	Output tax must be charged on all sales made by a registered trader.		
2	VAT is suffered by the final consumer.		
3	Registered traders making zero-rated supplies cannot recover any input tax.		

 Reference material

Some information about the scope of VAT, taxable and exempt supplies can be found in the 'Rates of VAT' and 'Partial exemption for VAT' sections of your reference material provided in the real assessment, so you do not need to learn it.

Why not look up the correct part of the reference material in the introduction to this text book now?

3 Tax point (time of supply)

3.1 Introduction

 Definition

The **tax point** is the date on which the liability for output tax arises. It is the date on which a supply is recorded as taking place for the purposes of the VAT return. It is also referred to as the **time of supply**.

Most taxable persons complete a VAT return each quarter. The return must include all supplies whose tax points fall within that quarter.

If the rate of VAT changes then all supplies with a tax point up to the date of change will be at the old rate and all supplies on or after the date of change will be at the new rate.

3.2 The basic tax point

The **basic tax point** for goods is the date when goods are 'removed' which usually means the date of delivery of those goods or the date the customer takes the goods away.

A tax point also occurs if goods are not 'removed' but are made available to a customer – for example if a specialist installer is constructing a new machine for a customer on site in their factory, the tax point will occur when the machine is handed over and not when all the materials are delivered to the site.

For services, the tax point is the date the services are performed or completed.

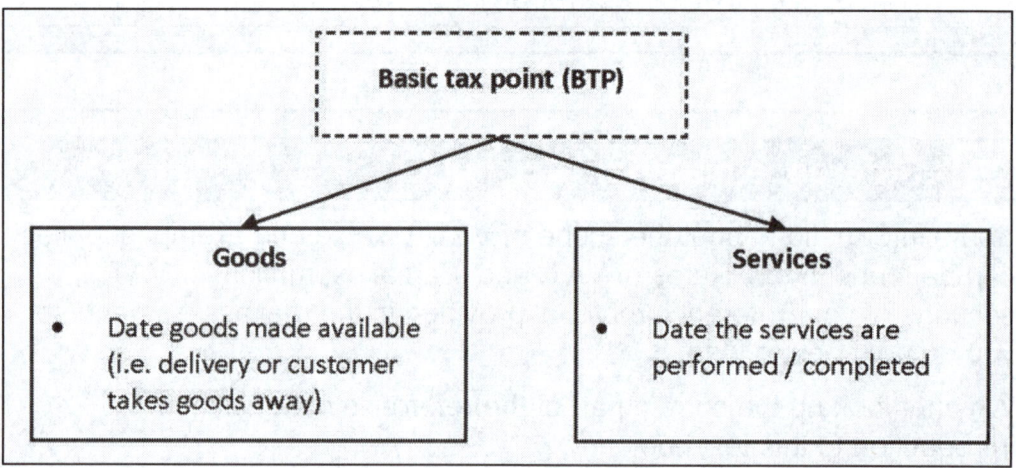

 Example

Queue Ltd received an order for goods from a customer on 14 March. The goods were despatched on 18 March and the customer paid on 15 April when the invoice dated 13 April was received.

State the basic tax point date.

Solution

The basic tax point is 18 March (i.e. the date of despatch).

3.3   Actual tax point

The basic tax point is amended in two situations.

Earlier tax point	Later tax point
• A tax invoice is issued or a payment is received on, or before, the basic tax point • In these circumstances the date of invoice or payment (whichever is earlier) is the time when the supply is treated as taking place	• A tax invoice is issued within 14 days after the basic tax point (14-day rule) (section 3.4) • In these circumstances the date of issue of the invoice is the time when the supply is treated as taking place

Note that an invoice is not issued until it has been sent or given to the customer.

3.4   The 14-day rule

If the earlier tax point does not apply, then the later tax point can be considered. If the invoice is issued within 14 days of the basic tax point the invoice date becomes the actual tax point.

If written approval is received from the VAT Written Enquiries Team, the 14-day rule in respect of issuing tax invoices can be varied.

For example, with agreement, it can be extended to accommodate a supplier who

- usually issues all invoices each month on the last day of the month, and

- would like the month end invoice date to be the tax point date.

However, where applicable, always apply the 14-day rule in your assessment unless the question suggests an extension has been agreed.

Note that the 14-day rule cannot apply to invoices that are only for zero-rated goods. These are not 'VAT invoices' because 0% is not a positive rate of VAT and so are disregarded for time of supply purposes.

For zero-rated supplies the tax point is the earlier of:

- when the goods are made available, and

- the receipt of payment.

Exports of taxable goods are zero-rated (Chapter 7), so the tax point for these goods is always the earlier of:

- the supply of goods (when the goods are sent to the customer), and

- the receipt of payment.

3.5 Identification of the tax point date

The procedure to identify the actual tax point date is as follows:

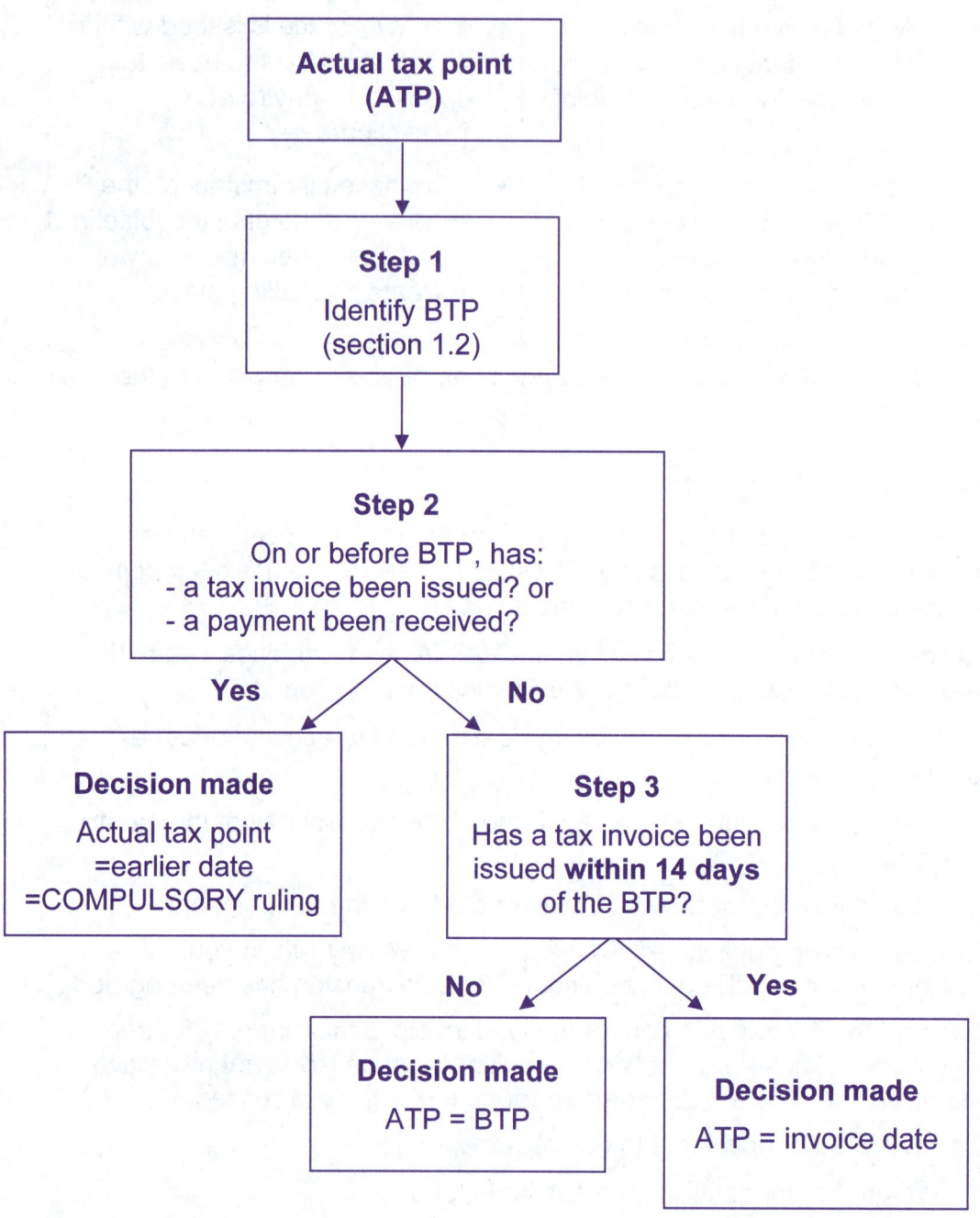

Test your understanding 6

In each of the following cases, state the tax point date.

		Tax point
1	Goods delivered to a customer on 15 August, invoice sent out on 20 August and payment received 30 August.	
2	Payment received with order from customer on 8 September, goods delivered on 13 September and invoice sent out on 30 September.	
3	Goods delivered to a customer on 4 March, invoice sent out on 25 March and payment received 15 April.	
4	Invoice sent to a customer on 10 December, goods delivered 18 December and payment received 27 December.	

 Reference material

Information about tax points can be found in the 'Tax points for VAT' section of your reference material provided in the real assessment, so you do not need to learn it.

Why not look up the correct part of the reference material in the introduction to this text book now?

3.6 Deposits received in advance

If a business receives a deposit or part payment in advance, then this creates a tax point when the deposit is received. A deposit may be made to reserve an item, for example, before the business supplies the goods or service.

However, this is only for the deposit, not the whole supply. The business must account for the VAT included in the deposit.

If a customer requires an invoice for a deposit or advance part payment, this is known as a pro-forma invoice. (Chapter 3) A pro-forma invoice does not create a tax point.

No tax point is created for a returnable deposit, where the deposit will be returned to the customer when the item is brought back safely (e.g. a deposit required to ensure the safe return of a hired item).

 Example

Ahmed receives a £60 deposit from a customer on 1 July.

The total cost of the item is £210 including VAT at 20% and the customer pays the balance of £150 on 12 September when they collect the goods. On 15 September, Ahmed issues an invoice to his customer, which he marks as paid in full.

How is VAT accounted for on this transaction?

Solution

Paying the deposit of £60 created a tax point on 1 July (as the payment date is before the goods are collected).

The amount of VAT is £10 (£60 × 20/120) and this must be entered in the VAT return that includes 1 July.

When the goods were collected and paid for on 12 September this created a further tax point (as the payment date is on the same day as the goods are collected).

The VAT is £25 (£150 × 20/120) and this must be included in the VAT return that includes 12 September.

The invoice date is not important as payment was made at the time the goods were removed (i.e. on the basic tax point date).

Test your understanding 7

In each of the following cases, state the tax point date.

		Tax point
1	Goods delivered to a customer on 10 July, tax invoice sent out on 15 July and payment received 30 July.	
2	Tax invoice sent out to a customer on 12 August, goods delivered to the customer on 16 August, payment received 20 September.	
3	Payment received from customer on 4 September, goods sent to customer on 5 September with a tax invoice dated on that day.	
4	Pro-forma invoice issued 3 June, payment received 10 June, and goods delivered 30 June with a tax invoice dated on that day.	

Test your understanding 8

A VAT registered business receives a £100 non-refundable deposit on 19 October from a customer for the supply of goods, which are despatched on 25 October.

The goods are invoiced on 31 October and the balance of £350 is paid on 10 November.

Both amounts are VAT-inclusive.

1   What is the tax point for the deposit?

    A   19 October

    B   25 October

    C   31 October

    D   10 November

2   What is the output VAT on the deposit?

    A   £20.00

    B   £16.67

3 What is the tax point for the balance?

A   19 October

B   25 October

C   31 October

D   10 November

4 What is the output VAT on the balance?

A   £70.00

B   £58.33

3.7   Goods on sale or return

Sometimes a customer may be sent goods on approval with a specified period in which to decide to keep the goods or return them.

Until the customer decides to keep the goods (referred to as 'adopting the goods'), they belong to the supplier and no VAT is due.

However, this situation could be exploited by giving the customer an artificially long period before the goods need to be accepted or returned.

Accordingly, the tax point rules stop goods being held for more than a year without VAT being due.

The basic tax point therefore occurs at the earliest of:

- the date the goods are adopted
- the date payment is received (except for refundable deposits)
- expiration of the time limit for adopting the goods
- 12 months from the date the goods were despatched.

Example

Reesha sells jewellery on a sale or return basis. Customers are given 90 days to decide to accept or return the goods.

Jewellery with a VAT-exclusive value of £670 is sent to Mike on 1 August 2024. He decides to buy the goods on 25 October 2024 and notifies Reesha on that date. Reesha receives payment from him on 7 November 2024.

The tax point is 25 October 2024, as this is the date the goods are adopted and is earlier than the expiry of the fixed time limit.

If Mike had not notified Reesha but simply sent the payment, then the tax point would be the 29 October 2024 as this is the date the fixed time period expires.

3.8 Continuous supplies

Some services are performed over a long period but are invoiced at regular intervals, rather than when the service has been completed (e.g. the leasing of equipment or the provision of utilities, such as gas and electricity).

If services are performed on a continuous basis with payments received regularly or from time to time, there is a tax point each time there is a payment, which is the **earlier of**:

- the date a VAT invoice is issued, or
- the date a payment is received.

If payments are due to be made at regular intervals (for example, by standing order or direct debit), a VAT invoice can be issued at the start of any period of up to one year (provided that more than one payment is due in the period) to cover all the payments due in that period.

For each payment, the business should set out the following:

- VAT-exclusive amount
- date on which the payment is due
- rate of VAT
- VAT payable.

In this case, the supplying business (i.e. the business issuing the invoice) does not have to pay all the output VAT to HMRC at the start of the year.

It will account for the tax on the earlier of:

- the payment due date for each regular payment, or

- the date payment is received.

The customer can reclaim input tax at the same time.

 Reference material

Information about continuous supplies and goods on sale or return can be found in the 'Tax points for VAT' section of your reference material provided in the real assessment, so you do not need to learn it.

Why not look up the correct part of the reference material in the introduction to this text book now?

 **HM Revenue and Customs**

4.1 Introduction

HM Revenue and Customs (HMRC) is the government body that is responsible for administering VAT.

VAT offices across the country are responsible for the local administration of VAT within a particular geographical area.

Local VAT offices deal with the collection of outstanding tax and carry out visits to taxpayers to check that they are complying with VAT rules.

HMRC are also responsible for dealing with all other issues concerning VAT including registration and record keeping (Chapter 2).

4.2 HMRC powers

HMRC have certain powers that help it administer VAT. These include:

- inspecting premises

- examining records

- making assessments for underpaid tax

- charging penalties for breaches of VAT rules (Chapter 7)

- determining whether certain supplies are liable for VAT.

Test your understanding 9

Which one of the following is NOT a power of HMRC?

A   Inspecting premises

B   Completing a business's VAT return

C   Examining records

D   Determining whether certain supplies are liable for VAT

4.3   Visits by VAT officers

VAT officers can visit premises to inspect records and make checks to ensure a business is paying or reclaiming the correct amount of VAT. A business will be contacted to arrange the visit and normally given 7 days' notice. (Chapter 2).

4.4   Assessments

A HMRC officer will issue an assessment if a trader has not submitted its VAT return by the due date (Chapter 5), or if the return has been submitted and it is incomplete or incorrect.

An assessment should usually be issued within two years of the relevant VAT period, extended to up to four years if new evidence comes to light. However this increases to 20 years if this is found to be as a result of deliberate conduct.

The trader has 30 days to appeal the assessment.

4.5   Disputes with HMRC

Most disagreements between the taxpayer and HMRC are resolved quickly, but if an agreement cannot be reached then the taxpayer has a choice of actions.

1   Ask for the case to be reviewed by another HMRC officer who has not previously been involved with the matter.

2   If the taxpayer does not wish the case to be reviewed by another officer, or disagrees with the review findings, the taxpayer can appeal to the Tax Tribunal. Such appeals are made initially to the First-tier Tax Tribunal. If the matter cannot be resolved there it may be appealed upwards to the Upper Tribunal and from there to the Court of Appeal and then the UK Supreme Court.

5 Summary

In this introductory chapter, we have looked at some of the basic principles and terminology used when dealing with VAT.

You should now understand that VAT is an indirect tax borne by the final consumer but collected on behalf of the government by businesses.

An important area covered in this chapter is the distinction between taxable and exempt supplies. Businesses making only exempt supplies cannot register for VAT or reclaim input tax.

The tax point for a supply of goods is important as this determines the VAT period in which the VAT on those goods is included. The basic tax point is the date on which goods are delivered or collected by a customer but there are also situations in which the tax point can be earlier or later. These rules must be understood.

The special rules for continuous supplies and goods on sale or return must also be understood.

HMRC is the UK's tax authority that controls VAT and has important powers you need to understand, including their right to visits to premises and inspecting records.

Test your understanding answers

 Test your understanding 1

The correct answer is C.

 Test your understanding 2

1   False – VAT is an indirect tax.

2   True – VAT is charged on business transactions so the statement is correct. Jake does not need to charge VAT on the sale of his bicycle.

3   False – Businesses collect VAT on behalf of the government so this statement is incorrect.

4   False – As Fred's business is registered for VAT he must account to HMRC for any output VAT charged to his customers.

 Test your understanding 3

1   £78.75 (£472.50 × 20/120)

2   £1,050.00 (£5,250 × 20%)

3   £211.50 (£4,230 × 5%)

4   £204.00 (£4,284 × 5/105)

 Test your understanding 4

1   Cannot

2   Taxable

3   Can
    Cannot

 Test your understanding 5

1 False – some sales may be exempt

2 True

3 False – zero-rated supplies are taxable supplies so VAT can be recovered on purchases and expenses incurred.

Test your understanding 6

1 20 August.

The invoice is raised within 14 days of the delivery date (the basic tax point) and hence a later tax point is created.

2 8 September.

The payment was received before delivery, so this creates an earlier tax point.

3 4 March.

The invoice is raised more than 14 days after the delivery date, so the tax point remains the same as the basic tax point of the delivery date.

4 10 December.

The goods are invoiced before delivery, so this creates an earlier tax point.

Test your understanding 7

1 15 July – invoice within 14 days after basic tax point
   (i.e. the delivery date 10 July)

2 12 August – goods invoiced before delivery

3 4 September – payment received before delivery

4 10 June – The issue of the pro-forma invoice is ignored so the receipt of payment is the tax point (as payment is received before delivery).

Test your understanding 8

1 The correct answer is A.
Receipt of cash on 19 October creates a tax point.

2 The correct answer is B.
£100 is VAT-inclusive so the VAT element is £16.67 (£100 × 1/6)

3 The correct answer is C.
The goods are invoiced within 14 days of delivery so a later tax point is created.

4 The correct answer is B.
£350 is VAT-inclusive so the VAT element is £58.33 (£350 × 1/6)

 Test your understanding 9

The correct answer is B.

A, C and D are all powers of HMRC.

VAT registration

Introduction

This chapter introduces the rules for both compulsory and voluntary VAT registration. It also explains when a business must deregister.

If a business does not register for VAT as soon as it starts trading, then the level of taxable turnover (standard, reduced and zero-rated supplies) must be monitored, to avoid missing the deadline for registration.

Remember from Chapter 1 that a taxable person is one who is, or who should be, registered for VAT. This means that even if a trader does not register when they should do, they may still have a liability for VAT and they may be charged a penalty.

It is important for a business to keep the correct records both for their business and for VAT purposes. This is dealt with in this chapter.

ASSESSMENT CRITERIA	CONTENTS
UK tax law principles relating to VAT (1.1)	1 Compulsory registration
	2 Consequences of registration
VAT registration and deregistration requirements (1.2)	3 Voluntary registration
	4 Deregistration
	5 Record keeping

1 Compulsory registration

1.1 Introduction

Not all businesses need to register for VAT, even if they make taxable supplies. Only businesses that have taxable supplies exceeding the registration threshold must register under the compulsory registration rules.

There are two separate tests for compulsory registration:

- Historic turnover test
- Future turnover test.

1.2 Turnover for registration purposes

Turnover for VAT registration purposes comprises of taxable supplies.

Taxable supplies for this purpose:

- includes all taxable supplies (standard, reduced and zero-rated), but
- excludes output VAT, and
- excludes sales of capital assets.

Exempt supplies are not included in turnover for the purposes of deciding whether a business should register for VAT.

1.3 Historic test

At the end of every calendar month, the trader must look at the cumulative total of taxable supplies for the last 12 months (or since starting in business if this is less than 12 months ago).

If the total exceeds the registration threshold of £90,000, the trader must register as follows.

- Notify HMRC **within 30 days** of the end of the month in which the turnover threshold is exceeded.

  Notification can be made either online or by post.

- Registration is effective from the **first day of the second month** after the turnover exceeded the threshold, or an agreed earlier date.

- A trader need not register if taxable supplies for the next 12 months are expected to be less than the deregistration threshold of £88,000 (Section 4).

  This helps businesses whose annual turnover is usually below the registration threshold, but have experienced one particularly good year.

Reference material

Information about registration thresholds can be found in the 'Registration and deregistration for VAT' section of your reference material provided in the real assessment, so you do not need to learn it.

Why not look up the correct part of the reference material in the introduction to this study text now?

 Example

Tariq started in business on 1 January 2024. His taxable turnover is £11,000 per month.

He checks his taxable turnover at the end of each month and discovers at the end of September 2024 that his taxable supplies for the previous 9 months have exceeded the registration threshold. (He will actually exceed during September but the test is only performed at each month-end.)

He must notify HMRC by 30 October 2024 and will be registered with effect from 1 November 2024, or an agreed earlier date.

 Test your understanding 1

Deanna starts a business on 1 June 2024.

Her monthly turnover of taxable supplies is £9,120.

1   When does Deanna have to notify HMRC of her liability to register and from which date would she normally be registered?

2   Would your answer to (1) be any different if Deanna's turnover was made up of half standard-rated and half zero-rated supplies? Why?

3   Would your answer to (1) be any different if Deanna's turnover was made up wholly of exempt supplies? Why?

1.4 Future test

A liability to register will also arise if taxable supplies within the next 30 days alone are expected to exceed the registration threshold of £90,000. This test is applied at any time, not just the end of a month.

- HMRC must be notified **before the end** of the 30 day period.
- Registration will be effective from the **beginning** of the 30 day period.

 Example

Dog Ltd signs a lease for new business premises on 1 June 2024 and opens for business on 15 September 2024. The company estimates that taxable supplies will be £95,000 per month starting immediately.

When does Dog Ltd have to register for VAT and notify HMRC?

Solution

Dog Ltd is liable to register for VAT because taxable supplies for the 30 days to 14 October 2024 are expected to exceed £90,000.

The company must notify HMRC of its liability to register by 14 October 2024 and is registered with effect from 15 September 2024.

Note: Dog Ltd does not make any taxable supplies before September 2024 so does not need to register before that date.

 Test your understanding 2

Ahmed has been in business for several years. He makes only standard-rated supplies, but is not yet registered for VAT.

His monthly turnover is £6,900. On 1 June 2024, he accepts an order with a sales value of £92,000 to be delivered at the end of June.

Which one of the following statements about Ahmed's VAT registration is correct?

A   The taxable turnover for the last 12 months is below the registration threshold so Ahmed is not yet required to register.

B   Ahmed will exceed the registration threshold at the end of June 2024 so will be registered from the start of August 2024.

C   Ahmed must register without delay because the new order is for an amount exceeding the VAT threshold.

Test your understanding 3

State which of the following unregistered traders are liable to register for VAT and the effective date of registration.

Name	Supplies	Details
Majid	Accountancy services (standard-rated)	Started in business on 1 October 2024. Estimated fees of £19,200 per month.
Jane	Clothing (standard and zero-rated)	Established the business on 1 July 2024 when Jane signed a contract to supply a local retailer. Sales for July 2024 are expected to be £105,000.
Sayso Ltd	Insurance broker (exempt)	Commenced trading 2 August 2024 with expected sales of £97,000 per month.
Omar	Stationers (standard-rated)	Has traded for many years with a normal turnover of around £78,000. A one-off successful month in July 2024 made total sales for the 12 months ended 31 December 2024 £91,000. Sales have since reverted to normal levels and are expected to continue at the same level.

 Test your understanding 4

You are given the following information about the taxable supplies of four businesses.

For each of the businesses select whether they need to register for VAT immediately, or monitor turnover and register later.

Tick one box on each line.

		Register now	Monitor and register later
1	A new business with an expected taxable turnover of £94,000 per month for the next 12 months.		

2	An existing business with a total taxable turnover of £75,200 since it began trading 11 months ago. The taxable turnover for the next month is not known.		
3	An existing business with a taxable turnover of £7,610 per month for the last 12 months.		
4	An existing business with a taxable turnover of £6,250 per month since it began trading six months ago. This is expected to increase to £9,300 per month for the next six months.		

 Test your understanding 5

Sohail commenced in business on 1 February 2024 making only taxable supplies. His turnover was as follows:

First 6 months to 31 July 2024 £5,250 per month

Next 12 months to 31 July 2025 £8,390 per month

1 On which of the following dates does Sohail exceed the registration threshold?

A 31 January 2025

B 28 February 2025

C 31 March 2025

D 30 April 2025

2 Select the date by which Sohail should notify HMRC that he has exceeded the registration threshold.

A 2 March 2025

B 30 March 2025

C 30 April 2025

D 30 May 2025

1.5 Number of registrations

A 'person' is registered for VAT. A 'person' is an individual, partnership or company.

An individual sole trader has only one registration, and this registration includes all the sole trader businesses that the individual carries on.

Where a partnership is concerned, a separate registration is required for the partnership. Other unincorporated businesses carried on by the individual partners will have a separate registration.

However, if the same partners are involved in multiple partnerships together, all of the businesses will fall under one single VAT registration.

Companies are all registered individually although it is possible for companies in certain sorts of groups to have a group registration. You do not need to know any details of this.

If one company takes over another company then they both continue with their individual registrations, unless they opt for a group registration.

If an unincorporated business is sold to a company, then the registration of the unincorporated business will cease, unless the company is not yet registered, in which case it may be possible to transfer the registration to the company.

 Example

Jason is a sole trader. He owns a clothing shop "Jason's Style" which is open during the day. In the evenings, he runs a business organising parties. Both businesses have a turnover of £47,000.

Jason is also a partner in Bash and Co, an import/export business he helps run with his wife. The partnership business has a turnover of £100,000.

Assuming the entire turnover of all of the businesses consists of taxable supplies, how many VAT registrations are required?

Solution

There are two registrations needed here:

(a)　One registration is needed to cover Jason's two sole trader businesses.

　　　Even though each business has taxable turnover below the registration threshold, the combined taxable turnover of the businesses is over the threshold.

(b)　One registration will cover Bash and Co, the partnership.

Test your understanding 6

Naina runs three sole trader businesses and is also in partnership with her husband running a fourth business.

Each of the businesses has taxable supplies exceeding the VAT registration threshold.

How many VAT registrations are required?

A   1

B   2

C   3

D   4

1.6   Exemption from registration

A trader making zero-rated supplies **only,** can apply for exemption from registration.

However, this would mean they cannot recover their input tax, and so the exemption is only likely to be applied for if:

- the trader does not want the administrative burden of complying with VAT regulations, or

- they do not have much input tax to recover.

2   Consequences of registration

2.1   Accounting for VAT

Once registered, a taxable person must start accounting for VAT.

- Output tax must be charged on taxable supplies and tax invoices must be issued to other registered traders

- Each registered trader is allocated a 9-digit VAT registration number, which must be quoted on all invoices. The business will also be advised of the VAT registration date. This is important to know so that output VAT is correctly charged and input VAT correctly accounted for in the first VAT return.

- Each registered trader is allocated a tax period for filing returns, which is normally every three months and usually fits in with their accounting year end. If required, the trader can request a particular return period.

- Input tax on most business purchases and expenses can be recovered. This can also include certain input VAT incurred before registration. Some exceptions are dealt with in Chapter 4.

- Appropriate VAT records must be kept (section 5).

Traders will be sent a certificate of registration, which contains their registration number and is proof of registration.

2.2 Changes to registration details

Certain changes to business details must be notified to HMRC within a certain timescale, otherwise a penalty may be charged.

This can be done either online or by post.

Change to be made	HMRC must be notified:
Name, trading name or address	Within 30 days
Partnership members	Within 30 days
Agent's details	Within 30 days
Bank account details	14 days in advance
Change in business activity	Within 30 days

2.3 Failure to register

If a trader does not register for VAT when the business's turnover exceeds the compulsory registration threshold, there are two consequences.

(i) All the VAT that the trader **should have charged** from the date they **should have registered** is payable to HMRC.

(ii) A penalty can be charged, which is a percentage of the VAT due – Chapter 7.

Traders have a choice when calculating the VAT, they should have charged.

They can either:

(i) treat their sales as VAT-inclusive and suffer the cost of the VAT themselves, or

(ii) add VAT to the invoice costs and try to recover this from their customers.

Option (ii) is unlikely as customers are under no obligation to pay this VAT. This means that the business will have to pay the VAT to HMRC out of its own profits.

This illustrates how important it is to keep up-to-date and monitor turnover.

 Example

Beverley runs a business manufacturing silicon cookware, which is a standard-rated supply.

On 1 October 2024, whilst talking to a friend, she realises she should have been registered since 1 March 2024 and immediately contacts HMRC. Her turnover since that date is £27,000 and she has suffered input VAT of £3,000 in that time.

The invoices will normally be treated as VAT-inclusive, so she will have to pay VAT to HMRC of £1,500 ((£27,000 × 20/120) − £3,000).

This VAT will be a cost to the business.

---

3 Voluntary registration

3.1 Actual or intending traders

Even if a person is not required to register, they can register provided they are **making or intending to make taxable supplies**.

HMRC will register the trader from the date of the request for voluntary registration, or a mutually agreed earlier date.

Remember that a trader who makes exempt supplies only, cannot register.

3.2 Advantages and disadvantages of voluntary registration

Advantages	Disadvantages
Avoids penalties for late registration.	Business will have to comply with the VAT administration rules, which may take time away from running the business.
Can recover input VAT on purchases and expenses.	Business must charge VAT. This makes their goods more expensive than an unregistered trader selling the same items or services. This extra cost cannot be recovered by unregistered customers such as the general public.
Can disguise the small size of the business.	

 Example

Luna sells wedding dresses, which would be standard-rated if she were registered for VAT. All of her sales are to members of the public. Her current annual turnover is £72,000.

Due to the competitive nature of her business, Luna is unable to increase her prices to the public.

If Luna registered for VAT she would be required to charge her customers output VAT. As she is unable to increase her prices her VAT-inclusive turnover would be £72,000 and she would have to account for output VAT to HMRC of £12,000 (£72,000 × 20/120). Her profits would therefore decrease by £12,000. However she would also be able to recover any input tax on purchases and so reduce her costs.

 Test your understanding 7

Which one of the following is a valid reason for a business making taxable supplies to choose to register voluntarily?

A   Preparation of VAT returns would be optional

B   The business would be able to reclaim input VAT

C   It would make their prices cheaper to the general public

D   It would make their prices cheaper to VAT-registered customers

4 Deregistration

4.1 Compulsory deregistration

A person **must** deregister when the business ceases to make taxable supplies.

- HMRC should be notified within 30 days of ceasing to make taxable supplies.
- VAT registration is cancelled from the date of cessation or a mutually agreed later date.

4.2 Voluntary deregistration

A person **may** voluntarily deregister, even if the business continues to trade, if taxable supplies in the next 12 months are not expected to exceed the deregistration threshold.

Although, a trader does not have to deregister if their sales fall below the deregistration threshold.

The deregistration threshold is always slightly lower than the registration threshold, and is currently £88,000.

- The 12-month period can start at any time. It does not have to be the beginning or end of a month.
- The trader must prove to HMRC that they qualify.
- VAT registration is cancelled from the date of the request, or an agreed later date.

Test your understanding 8

Assuming that the registration threshold is £90,000, indicate whether the following statements are true or false. Tick one box on each line.

		True	False
1	An unregistered trader can never have a VAT liability to HMRC.		
2	A trader making taxable supplies only, of £50,000 per annum cannot register for VAT.		
3	A trader making exempt supplies only, of £100,000 per annum must register for VAT.		
4	A trader's VAT registration number must be quoted on all sales invoices.		
5	A registered trader must deregister if their taxable supplies fall below the deregistration threshold.		

4.3 Effect of deregistration

On deregistration, the trader will no longer charge output VAT and no longer reclaim input VAT.

Output tax must be paid to HMRC on the value of capital assets and inventory owned at the date of deregistration, unless the VAT due on these assets is no more than £1,000.

This takes back the input tax relief that the business would have had when it bought those assets.

Test your understanding 9

(a) Jig Ltd closed down its business on 10 October 2024.

State when Jig Ltd should notify HMRC of the business cessation and from when the business will be deregistered.

(b) At 1 May 2024, Eli thinks that his taxable turnover for the year to 30 April 2025 will be below the deregistration threshold. He immediately applies for deregistration.

State when Eli will be deregistered.

 Reference material

Information about deregistration thresholds can be found in the 'Registration and deregistration for VAT' section of your reference material provided in the real assessment, so you do not need to learn it.

Why not look up the correct part of the reference material in the introduction to this text book now?

 Test your understanding 10

You are given the following information about four traders. Identify whether or not the trader **must** register for VAT.

Tick one box on each line.

		Yes	No
1	A trader making zero-rated supplies only, of £110,000 per annum.		
2	A trader who has taxable supplies of £91,000 for the last 12 months, but who expects to make only £65,000 of taxable supplies in the next 12 months.		
3	An unincorporated trader who runs two separate businesses making standard-rated supplies of £47,000 each.		

4	An unincorporated trader who runs two separate businesses making annual standard-rated supplies of £73,000 in one business and annual exempt supplies of £22,000 in the other.		

5   Record keeping

5.1   General requirements

Businesses must keep information that will allow the business to calculate VAT correctly and allow HMRC to check VAT returns adequately.

Generally, the business must keep records of:

- all taxable and exempt supplies made in the course of business

- all taxable supplies received in the course of business

- the total output tax and input tax for each tax period – the VAT account (Chapter 6).

Failure to keep records can lead to a penalty. (Chapter 7)

The business must keep records to prove the figures shown on the VAT returns for the previous **six** years, although HMRC can reduce this period where the records are bulky and the information they contain can be provided in another way.

Records may be stored electronically, particularly if this facilitates easier storage and access. There is no requirement for all records to be kept at business headquarters at all times, but they must be readily available to HMRC during an enquiry.

 Reference material

Information about record keeping deadlines can be found in the 'Keeping business and VAT records' section of your reference material provided in the real assessment, so you do not need to learn it.

Why not look up the correct part of the reference material in the introduction to this text book now?

5.2   Business records

Records need to be kept for business purposes and for VAT purposes.

Business records that should be kept are:

- annual accounts including statements of profit or loss (income statements)
- bank statements paying-in slips and cheque stubs
- cash books and other account books
- orders and delivery notes
- purchases and sales day books
- recordings of daily takings, including till rolls
- relevant business correspondence.

5.3   VAT records

VAT records are needed to allow the calculation of amounts owed to HMRC or due from HMRC in each VAT period.

Records do not have to be kept in any particular way. However, it must be possible for HMRC to check the records and confirm how the figures in the VAT return have been calculated.

However, the records that form part of the 'electronic account' **must** be kept digitally. (Section 5.4)

Records that should be kept include:

- records of all the standard-rated, reduced-rated, zero-rated and exempt goods and services that the business buy or sell
- purchase invoices (Chapter 3) (Note this is not necessary for purchases of £25 or less purchased through a coin operated machine, e.g. car parking)
- copy sales invoices (Chapter 3)
- any credit or debit notes issued or received (Chapter 3)
- records of goods and services bought for which you cannot reclaim VAT
- import and export documents
- any adjustments or corrections to your VAT account or VAT invoices
- a VAT account.

5.4   Electronic VAT records

Businesses must keep digital VAT records. (Chapter 6)

Registered businesses may be visited by a VAT officer on occasion to ensure that their records are being correctly maintained. It must make sure that the records are easily accessible if a VAT officer visits.

6 Summary

In this chapter, we have considered which traders need to become VAT-registered and the effects of registration.

Both the historic and future test for registration have been set out. Remember that it is the turnover of taxable supplies, including zero-rated supplies, that determines whether a business needs to register for VAT.

It is also important to remember that businesses that only make exempt supplies **cannot** register for VAT whilst businesses that **only** make **zero-rated** supplies **need not** register for VAT if they do not wish to do so.

Failure to register when taxable supplies have exceeded the threshold can cost a business a great deal.

Firstly, they must pay over the VAT they should have collected from customers and secondly they may be charged a penalty.

Traders can choose to register voluntarily provided they are making taxable supplies now or intend to in the future.

This allows the business to recover input tax, but may make the price of their goods comparatively more expensive than those of an unregistered trader.

We learnt that a business **must** deregister if it ceases to make taxable supplies, and **may** deregister if its taxable supplies for the next 12 months will be below the deregistration threshold.

Finally, all VAT registered businesses are required to keep their VAT records in digital form and must provide their VAT return through HMRC MTD-compatible software.

Test your understanding answers

Test your understanding 1

1   Deanna's taxable turnover will exceed £90,000 after 10 months, which is at the end of March 2025. She must notify HMRC by 30 April 2025 and will be registered with effect from 1 May 2025.

2   No – taxable supplies includes both standard-rated and zero-rated supplies.

3   Yes – traders who only make exempt supplies cannot register for VAT.

Test your understanding 2

The correct answer is C.

Ahmed must register under the future test, as his taxable supplies in the next 30 days alone will exceed the registration threshold.

He must notify HMRC by 30 June 2024 and will be registered with effect from 1 June 2024.

Test your understanding 3

Majid will exceed the registration threshold after 5 months in business, that is, at the end of February 2025. He must notify HMRC by 30 March 2025 and will be registered from 1 April 2025.

Jane must register under the future test as her sales will immediately exceed the registration threshold within the next 30 days. She must notify HMRC by 30 July 2024 and will be registered from 1 July 2024.

Sayso Ltd cannot register as it only makes exempt supplies.

Omar's taxable supplies for the 12 months ended 31 December 2024 exceeded the threshold of £90,000. However, he does not expect his taxable supplies in the following 12 months to exceed the deregistration threshold of £88,000. Accordingly, Omar is not required to register.

Test your understanding 4

1   Register now – taxable turnover is expected to exceed the registration threshold in the next 30 days.

2   Monitor and register later – taxable turnover for the period to date does not exceed the registration threshold.

Note that if there has not yet been 12 months of trading, you do not time apportion the threshold. Just compare the taxable turnover of the shorter period to the full threshold.

3   Register now – taxable turnover has exceeded the registration threshold in the last 12 months.

4   Monitor and register later – taxable turnover has not yet exceeded the threshold.

 Test your understanding 5

1   The correct answer is D.

Taxable turnover for the first 12 months to 31 January is £81,840, then 12 months to 28 February £84,980 and to 31 March £88,120 and to 30 April £91,260.

2   The correct answer is D.

Traders must notify HMRC within 30 days of exceeding the threshold.

 Test your understanding 6

The correct answer is B.

Two registrations are needed. One is in respect of all of Naina's sole trade businesses, and another in respect of the partnership with her husband.

Test your understanding 7

The correct answer is B.

A is incorrect, as it would be compulsory to complete VAT returns.

C is incorrect, as the public would have to pay VAT that they could not recover.

D is incorrect, as VAT-registered customers would have to pay VAT on purchases, which they could then recover, such that the price of the goods and services to them is the same whether or not the supplier business chooses to be VAT-registered.

 Test your understanding 8

1   False – if a trader fails to register when they should, i.e. if they have exceeded the threshold, then they can be asked to pay over all the output VAT they should have charged.

2   False – traders making taxable supplies can register voluntarily.

3   False – traders making only exempt supplies cannot register for VAT.

4   True – the VAT registration number must be shown on all invoices.

5   False – traders only **have to** deregister if they cease to make taxable supplies. If their supplies fall below the deregistration threshold they can choose to deregister.

 Test your understanding 9

(a)   Jig Ltd must notify HMRC of their business cessation by 8 November 2024 (i.e. within 30 days including the date of cessation). The business will be deregistered from 10 October 2024 (i.e. date of cessation), or from a mutually agreed later date.

(b)   Eli's registration will be cancelled with effect from 1 May 2024 (i.e. date of request), or an agreed later date.

Test your understanding 10

1   No – businesses that only make zero-rated supplies can apply to be exempted from registration.

2   No – if a business exceeds the registration threshold it need not register if taxable turnover in the next 12 months will be below the deregistration threshold.

3   Yes – the taxable turnover of all of a trader's sole trader businesses are aggregated to determine whether the trader has exceeded the VAT threshold.

4   No – exempt supplies are not taken into account for registration.

VAT documentation

3

Introduction

This chapter looks at how VAT is collected via a VAT invoice and all the details that are required to be shown on an invoice. Other documents such as credit notes and pro-forma invoices are also covered.

It is important to know how to correctly account for VAT when discounts are offered, and understanding the importance of keeping staff up to date on changes in VAT legislation is discussed.

ASSESSMENT CRITERIA	CONTENTS
Extracting relevant data from accounting records (2.1)	1 VAT invoices
	2 Simplified and modified invoices
VAT invoices (2.2)	3 Discounts
VAT calculations (2.3)	4 Other documentation
Communicating information on VAT related matters (5.1)	5 Changes in VAT legislation
	6 Sources of information
	7 Keeping up to date with VAT

1 VAT invoices

1.1 Introduction

All businesses that are registered for VAT must provide evidence to VAT-registered customers of the VAT they have been charged.

In order to do this the supplier must give or send to the purchaser a VAT invoice **within 30 days** of the earlier of:

- supply of the goods or services, or
- receipt of the payment.

VAT invoices are not required:

- if the purchaser is not VAT-registered,
- if the supply is wholly zero-rated or exempt,
- where the seller is a retailer and it is a free sample of something that is usually subject to VAT

In practice, it is not always possible to tell if a purchaser is VAT registered or not, so traders normally issue a VAT invoice anyway, although retailers selling to the public do not have to issue a VAT invoice unless requested.

Traders will normally issue invoices for zero-rated sales, which show the same details as for other supplies, but technically this is not a VAT invoice.

The original VAT invoice is sent to the customer and forms the customer's evidence for reclaiming input VAT.

A copy must be kept by the supplier to support the calculation of output VAT.

1.2 Form of a VAT invoice

There is **no standard format for invoices**. The exact design is the choice of the business, but it must show the following details (unless the invoice is a **simplified tax invoice** or a **modified invoice**, explained later in the chapter):

- identifying number which must follow a sequence (if an invoice is spoilt or cancelled it must be kept as a VAT officer may wish to inspect it)
- supplier's name and address
- supplier's VAT registration number
- the date of issue of the invoice

- the date of supply (tax point) if different from the invoice date
- name and address of customer (i.e. the person to whom the goods or services are supplied)
- type of supply
    - sale
    - hire purchase, credit sale, conditional sale or similar transaction
    - loan or exchange
    - hire, lease or rental
    - process (making goods using the customer's own materials)
    - sale on commission (e.g. an estate agent)
    - supply on sale or return
- description of the goods or services
- unit price or rate, excluding VAT
- quantity of goods or extent of services
- rate of tax and amount payable excluding VAT for each separate description
- total amount payable (excluding VAT)
- rate of any cash discount offered (these are also called settlement discounts)
- separate rate and amount of VAT charged for each rate of VAT
- total amount of VAT chargeable (in sterling).

A VAT invoice does NOT have to include any other items such as:

- customer's order number

- date of order

- customer's VAT registration number

- method of delivery.

Invoices can be paper or electronic (e-invoice). If electronic, it must be in a secure format like a pdf.

 Reference material

Information about the contents of an invoice can be found in the 'Contents of a VAT invoice' section of your reference material provided in the real assessment, so you do not need to learn it.

Why not look up the correct part of the reference material in the introduction to this text book now?

1.3 Exempt or zero-rated supplies

If a business issues an invoice that includes zero-rated or exempt supplies, then the invoice must show clearly that there is no VAT on those items and their values must be totalled separately.

Alternatively, the business could issue separate invoices for zero-rated and for exempt supplies.

Note that separate invoices for only zero-rated or exempt supplies are not VAT invoices.

1.4   Example of a VAT invoice

The example invoice below shows the detail required for a valid tax invoice.

Example

MICRO TRAINING GROUP LTD
Unit 34, Castlewell Trading Estate
Manchester M12 5RHF

To: Slough Labels Ltd	Sales invoice number:	35
Station Unit	VAT registration number:	234 5566 87
Slough	Date of issue:	30 September 2024
SL1 3EJ	Tax point:	12 September 2024

Sales:

No.	Description and price	Amount excl VAT £	VAT rate	VAT £
6	Programmable calculators FR34 at £24.76	148.56	20%	29.71
12	Programmable calculators GT60 at £36.80	441.60	20%	88.32
		590.16		118.03
	Delivery	23.45	20%	4.69
		613.61		122.72
VAT		122.72		
TOTAL		736.33		

Terms: Net 30 days.

1.5   Rounding VAT

Usually, the amount of VAT calculated will not be a whole number of pounds and pence. You will therefore need a rounding adjustment. Mathematical rounding to the nearest penny is required.

Test your understanding 1

Calculate the total VAT to be charged in respect of each of the three VAT invoices below. State your answer rounded to the nearest penny.

Invoice	Description and price	Net of VAT £	VAT rate	VAT £
1	16 × 6 metre hosepipes @ £3.23 each	51.68	20%	
2	24 × bags of compost @ £5.78 each	138.72	20%	
3	Supply of kitchen units	1,084.57	20%	

2 Simplified and modified invoices

2.1 Simplified VAT invoices

Invoices with fewer details on them can be issued by any business, if the value of the supply is below a certain limit.

If the total amount of the supply **(including VAT)** does not exceed £250, then the business may issue a simplified invoice.

However, a full VAT invoice must be issued if a customer requests one.

The details required on the simplified invoice are:

- supplier's name and address
- supplier's VAT registration number
- date of supply (tax point)
- description sufficient to identify the goods or services
- amount payable (including VAT) for each rate
- the VAT rate applicable.

The main differences between a simplified invoice and a full invoice are that the customer's name and address can be omitted, an invoice number is not essential and the total on the invoice includes the VAT without the VAT itself being shown separately.

Although this invoice shows less detail, it is still a valid VAT invoice.

This means that if the purchaser is a VAT-registered business they can use the invoice to support a claim for input VAT.

 Example

Delta Office Supplies

46, Central Mall, Glastonbury, Somerset
G34 7QT
Telephone: 01392 43215
Tax point: 15 April 2024

1 × Box High-quality A4 copier paper
Stock no: 1276CY
Total including VAT @ 20%   £25.85

VAT registration number: 653 7612 44

If the business accepts credit cards, it can use the sales voucher given to the cardholder as a less detailed invoice.

However, it must still contain the details in this example.

 Test your understanding 2

Look at the following list of items.

Select by entering the appropriate number whether the items:

1   Should only be shown on a full VAT invoice; or

2   Should be shown on both a full VAT invoice and on a simplified invoice; or

3   Should not be shown on either form of invoice.

	Item	Number (1, 2, or 3)
A	Identifying number	
B	Tax point date	
C	Delivery date	
D	Total amount of VAT payable	
E	Customer's registration number	

Test your understanding 3

A manufacturing business, which is registered for VAT, sells both standard and zero-rated goods.

Which one of the following combinations of supplies can be shown on a simplified invoice?

	Standard-rated supplies	Zero-rated supplies
A	£200 + VAT	£30
B	£240 + VAT	Nil
C	£50 + VAT	£180

2.2 Modified VAT invoices

A modified invoice is a type of VAT invoice that includes the total price of the products and/or services inclusive of VAT.

It includes all the same details as a full VAT invoice with the exception of showing the VAT inclusive (rather than VAT exclusive) amounts for each product and/ or service supplied.

Modified invoices are only issued on products or services with a total amount over £250.

Modified invoices are generally issued by retailers as they usually sell products directly to consumers rather than other businesses.

Example

MACRO STATIONARY LTD
25 Repton Avenue
Newcastle NE1 1EN

To: Ethan Smith	Sales invoice number: 74
102 High lane	VAT registration number: 234 751434
London	Date of issue: 30 July 2024
SE7 4RF	Tax point: 12 July 2024

Sales:

Qty	Description and price	Amount excl VAT £	VAT rate	Amount incl VAT £
20	Staples (4 boxes) S12 at £12.45	249.00	20%	298.80
75	Paper 100gsm (6 reems) P54 at £24.97	1,872.75	20%	2,247.30
	Subtotal without VAT	2,121.75		2,546.10
	VAT 20% of	424.35		
	TOTAL	2,546.10		

Terms: Net 30 days.

Reference material

Information about full, simplified and modified invoices can be found in the 'Contents of a VAT invoice' section of your reference material provided in the real assessment, so you do not need to learn it.

Why not look up the correct part of the reference material in the introduction to this text book now?

2.3 Retention of invoices

All businesses must keep records of:

- all sales invoices issued except copies of simplified VAT invoices for items under £250 (including VAT)

- all purchase invoices for items purchased for business purposes unless the gross value of the supply is £25 (including VAT) or less, and the purchase was from a coin-operated telephone or vending machine, or for car parking charges or tolls.

Test your understanding 4

Indicate whether the following statements are true or false.

Tick one box on each line.

		True	False
1	Traders do not have to supply a VAT invoice unless their customer is VAT-registered.		
2	Businesses can issue simplified VAT invoices if the total amount of the supply, excluding VAT, does not exceed £250.		
3	The VAT invoice is used by a customer as evidence for reclaiming input VAT.		
4	A VAT invoice must be issued to a customer within 30 days of the tax point.		
5	A modified invoice includes all the same detail as a full invoice.		

3 Discounts

3.1 Trade discounts and bulk buy discounts

A trader may offer a **trade discount** to loyal customers and/or a **bulk buy discount** (or bulk quantity discount).

If this is the case, VAT is charged on the **discounted price**, not the full price of the goods or services.

 Example

Joachim is in business manufacturing angle brackets, which he sells to retailers.

He offers a 5% trade discount.

He sells angle brackets (a standard-rated supply) with a pre-discount price of £1,000 to Kim Ltd.

How much VAT should he charge on the invoice?

Solution

VAT should be calculated on the discounted price.

Accordingly, the VAT is £190.00 (£1,000 × 95% × 20%).

The amount of the VAT is fixed by what is on the invoice and this must be calculated on the discounted figure.

In the previous example:

- The supplier's OUTPUT tax and the customer's INPUT tax is £190.00.

- The customer will need a copy of the invoice to reclaim VAT and they can only reclaim £190.00.

Test your understanding 5

An invoice is issued for standard-rated goods with a list price of £380.00 (excluding VAT).

A 10% bulk buy discount is given.

How much VAT should be included on the invoice?

A   £76.00

B   £57.00

C   £68.40

D   £63.33

Sometimes a business will **offer to pay a customer's VAT**.

This is really just another form of discount.

VAT is calculated on the amount the customer would have paid on the discounted price, not the full price (i.e. the amount paid by the customer is treated as the VAT-inclusive amount).

 Example

XY Ltd sells beds with a normal retail price of £240 (which includes VAT of £40).

They run a promotional offer to pay the customers' VAT for them and hence the customer pays £200.

How much output VAT must XY Ltd account for?

Solution

XY Ltd must treat the £200 paid as a VAT-inclusive price and account for VAT of £33.33 (£200 × 1/6).

Test your understanding 6

Calculate the amount of output VAT that should be charged on the following invoices for standard-rated supplies.

State your answer rounded to the nearest penny.

	Output tax £
Pre-discounted price = £1,000 (VAT-exclusive) Trade discount of 10%	
Supplier offers to pay customer's VAT Amount paid = £2,500	
Pre-discounted price = £750 (VAT-exclusive) Bulk buy discount of 8%	

3.2 Prompt payment (cash or settlement) discounts

If a trader offers a discount for payment within a certain period, then VAT must be accounted for on the **actual** amount that the customer pays.

This causes difficulty for the supplier, as the supplier does not know in advance whether the customer will pay in time and be entitled to take the discount.

There are two ways that a trader can deal with this.

1   Invoice the customer for the full amount and charge VAT on the full amount.

   If the customer pays on time and takes the discount, then the trader can issue a credit note for the discount plus VAT.

   Note that if the VAT rate changes between the issue of the invoice and the credit note, then the original VAT rate must be used on the credit note.

2   Invoice for the full amount plus VAT but include on the invoice information about the discounted amount plus VAT.

   The customer then knows how much to pay if payment is made within the discount period.

   It must be made clear on the invoice that the customer can only recover the input tax actually paid.

   A warning should be included that claiming more VAT than the customer is entitled to is an offence.

Example

Perry Ltd offers customers a 5% prompt payment discount if they pay within 30 days. The company invoices customers the full amount and then issues a credit note for any discount.

Perry Ltd sells standard-rated goods worth £670 VAT-exclusive to Evans Ltd. Evans Ltd pays within 30 days so is entitled to the 5% discount.

Perry Ltd should invoice Evans Ltd for £804 (£670 plus £134 VAT at 20%).

Perry Ltd should then issue a credit note for £40.20 (£33.50 (5% of £670) plus of £6.70 VAT at 20%).

Perry Ltd must account for output VAT of £127.30 (£134.00 – £6.70). Evans Ltd can recover input VAT of £127.30.

Note that in an assessment, if you are just asked to calculate the discounted amount and the VAT, there is no need to do it in two stages.

You can calculate just as you do with trade and bulk buy discounts (i.e. input VAT recoverable = (£670 × 95% × 20%) = £127.30)

 Test your understanding 7

A trader issues an invoice to a customer for the following:

– standard-rated items of £220 plus VAT

– zero-rated items of £130

A prompt payment discount of 2% is available and is given through a credit note.

Assuming the customer takes the cash discount, how much input VAT will they be entitled to claim on the invoice less the credit note?

A   £44.00

B   £43.12

C   £36.66

D   £35.93

4 Other documentation

4.1 Credit notes

When customers return goods that were taxable supplies, the supplier may issue a credit note. This has to have similar information to that found on the original invoice and must be **labelled clearly as a credit note**.

The number and date of the original tax invoice should also appear on the credit note.

If the supplier issues the credit note without making a VAT adjustment, the credit note must say '**This is not a credit note for VAT**'.

A supplier is not allowed to issue a credit note to recover VAT on bad debts (i.e. irrecoverable debts).

From the supplier's point of view, the VAT on the credit note issued must be deducted from output VAT payable.

From the customer's point of view, the VAT on the credit note received must be deducted from input tax recoverable.

Alternatively, the supplier can cancel the original invoice and reissue it with the correct figures.

 Test your understanding 8

A business issues a sales credit note.

What is the effect on VAT?

A Output VAT will increase

B Output VAT will decrease

C Input VAT will increase

D Input VAT will decrease

4.2 Debit notes

If a customer returns goods, they can wait for:

- the supplier to reissue a corrected invoice, or

- the supplier to issue them with a credit note, or

- they can issue a debit note to their supplier.

Note that these are **alternatives** – you **cannot** account for both a debit note issued and a credit note received for the same supply.

From the supplier's point of view, the VAT on a debit note received from a customer must be deducted from output tax payable.

From the customer's point of view, the VAT on a debit note issued must be deducted from their input tax recoverable.

The treatment of the VAT can be summarised as follows:

	SELLER (supplier)	BUYER (customer)
Seller issues credit note	Deduct from output tax	Deduct from input tax
Buyer issues debit note	Deduct from output tax	Deduct from input tax
Effect	Reduce VAT payable	Increase VAT payable

 Test your understanding 9

A business issues a purchase debit note.

What is the effect on its VAT?

A   Output VAT will increase

B   Output VAT will decrease

C   Input VAT will increase

D   Input VAT will decrease

4.3 Pro-forma invoices

When a business issues a sales invoice that includes VAT, the VAT becomes payable to HMRC next time the business submits a return.

A business is therefore unlikely to issue a tax invoice before goods are despatched. This can cause cash flow problems if the customer has not yet paid the invoice, because the business then has to pay the VAT to HMRC before collecting it from their customers.

To avoid this, a business may issue a **pro-forma invoice** for goods or services not yet supplied, which essentially is an offer to supply goods and services and a request for payment.

Once the customer accepts the goods or services offered and/or a payment is received, the business will then issue a 'live' tax invoice to replace the pro-forma.

Because a pro-forma invoice does not rank as a VAT invoice the supplier is not required to pay VAT to HMRC until the 'live' tax invoice is issued.

For this reason, the customer cannot reclaim VAT on a pro-forma invoice but must instead wait until the valid VAT invoice is received.

Pro-forma invoices must be clearly marked with the words '**This is not a VAT invoice**'.

 Test your understanding 10

Which of the following statements about pro-forma invoices are FALSE?

Enter a tick in the final box for each false statement.

		False
A	A pro-forma invoice IS a valid tax invoice	
B	A pro-forma invoice IS NOT a valid tax invoice	
C	A customer receiving a pro-forma invoice can use it to reclaim the input tax shown	
D	A pro-forma invoice is really just an offer to supply goods and services and a request for payment	

4.4 Statements and demands for payment

It is important to appreciate that only VAT invoices and credit notes should be entered in the VAT records.

When a business sends out a demand for payment or a statement there is no VAT implications.

VAT has already been recorded and the demand or statement is simply the business trying to collect what it is owed.

4.5 Orders and delivery notes

These are also ignored for VAT and cannot be used by a customer as evidence for reclaiming VAT on their purchases.

4.6 VAT-only invoices

Sometimes a business needs to increase VAT charged on an earlier invoice or may have forgotten to include VAT.

One solution would be to credit the original invoice and then re-invoice it.

Alternatively, the business can issue an invoice just for the VAT and label it as a VAT-only invoice.

Such an invoice must be entered in the VAT records and the tax paid to HMRC as usual.

A registered purchaser who receives the invoice will treat it as a normal VAT invoice and be able to recover the VAT charged.

 Test your understanding 11

Refer to the three invoices set out below which have been received from suppliers during March 2024. No entries have yet been made in Hoddle Ltd's books of account in respect of these 3 documents.

You are required to state whether these are valid VAT invoices and how much input tax (if any) can be claimed in respect of these.

Engineering Supplies Limited

Haddlefield Road, Blaysley, CG6 6AW
Tel/Fax: 01376 44531

Hoddle Limited   **SALES INVOICE NO:** 2155
22 Formguard Street
Pexley
PY6 3QW

Date: 27 March 2024

	£
VAT omitted in error from invoice no 2139 dated 15 March 2024	
£2,667.30 @ 20%	533.46
Total due	533.46

Terms: net 30 days

VAT registration: 318 1827 58

Alpha Stationery

Aindsale Centre, Mexton, EV1 4DF
Telephone: 01392 43215

26 March 2024

	£
1 box transparent folders: red	
Total incl VAT @ 20%	14.84
Amount tendered	20.00
Change	5.16

VAT registration: 356 7612 33

JAMIESON & CO

Jamieson House, Baines Road, Gresham, GM7 2PQ
Telephone: 01677 35567   Fax: 01677 57640

PRO-FORMA SALES INVOICE

VAT registration: 412 7553 67

Hoddle Limited
22 Formguard Street
Pexley
PY6 3QW

For professional services in connection with debt collection

	£
Our fees	350.00
VAT	70.00
Total due	420.00

A VAT invoice will be submitted when the total due is paid in full.

	Valid VAT invoice	Input tax £
Engineering Supplies Ltd	YES/NO	
Alpha Stationery	YES/NO	
Jamieson and Co	YES/NO	

5 Changes in VAT legislation

5.1 Change in the rate of VAT

The tax point date becomes very important when there is a change in the rate of VAT or if a supply is reclassified from one rate of VAT to another.

Tax invoices with a tax point date before the change must use the old rate of VAT.

If they have a date on/after the change then they must use the new rate.

5.2 Effect of a VAT rate change on a business

A change in the rate of VAT has a major effect on the business accounting system including the following:

- Sales invoices need to be produced with the correct rate of VAT.

- Sales prices used in quotes or for pricing invoices must include the correct rate of VAT.

- Retail businesses need to make sure that prices displayed to the public are correct.

- Staff expense claims must reclaim the correct rate of VAT on (for example) mileage expenses.

- The correct input tax reclaim must be made for purchases and expenses.

    Input VAT claimed should be whatever figure is shown on the invoice for the purchase or expense.

    However, staff would need to know the details of any rate change so that they can query any actual errors with suppliers.

In a computerised system, the accounting software must be updated to produce sales invoices at the correct rate and to deal with differing rates of VAT on purchase invoices.

If the VAT is calculated at the point of sale by a till system, the system must be adjusted to take account of the new rate.

In both cases, it is important that the change occurs at the correct time. For example, new prices would need to be quoted to customers from the date of change.

However, sales invoices must use the rate of VAT relevant to the tax point date and not necessarily the date the invoice is raised.

5.3 Changing prices

Whether or not a change in VAT rate is passed on to the customer is a commercial decision for a business to make.

The current prices can be maintained and the cost of a VAT increase (or profit from a VAT decrease) can be absorbed by the business.

If the rate of VAT increases and the business does not pass on the increase to their customers, then they will have reduced cash flow as well as profit.

The opposite would be true if the VAT rate decreased and the business did not pass on the reduction to their customers.

5.4 Informing staff

A number of different staff within a business would need to be told about a rate change and its effects.

- IT department staff – to ensure the relevant changes are made to the computerised accounting system.

- Sales ledger staff – to raise or check sales invoices correctly.

- Purchase ledger staff – so that they can check purchase invoices correctly.

- Sales staff – to ensure customers are given correct prices.

- Marketing department staff – so that any new brochures or publicity material is correct.

- Staff generally – to ensure their expense claims are made correctly.

In your assessment, you may need to complete an email advising relevant people of the change, as shown in the following hypothetical example.

> ### 💡 Example
>
> To: Sales ledger staff
> From: Junior Accountant
> Subject: Change in the rate of VAT
> Date: 14/3/2024
>
> Please note that the standard rate of VAT, which applies to all our products, will change on 1 April 2024 from 20% to 22%.
>
> Any invoices with a tax point date of 1 April or later must have the new VAT rate applied.
>
> It is important that invoices with a tax point date before 1 April continue to include VAT at the old rate.

6 Sources of information

6.1 Legislation

The main source of law on VAT is the VAT Act 1994 as amended by annual Finance Acts and other regulations issued by Parliament.

6.2 GOV.UK website

HMRC expect taxpayers to be able to answer many of their queries by searching the HMRC section of the gov.uk website at:

https://www.gov.uk/government/collections/vat-detailed-information

HMRC publications can be searched online. Some sections are available as pdfs and can be downloaded.

Publications available include:

- VAT guide (VAT Notice 700)

- Information sheets on particular topics.

HMRC also provide educational and explanatory material online including:

- YouTube videos

- Live webinars with links to recordings of past webinars.

Businesses can also sign up to receive emails about VAT.

6.3 VAT guide

HMRC issue a booklet called the VAT guide (VAT Notice 700). This is the main guide to VAT rules and procedures. There are a number of supplements and amendments to the guide to keep it up to date.

The VAT guide is also available online on the HMRC section of the gov.uk website. As it is a large document (over 250 pages long), it is broken into sections on the website. It can be searched online or downloaded.

If you are dealing with accounting for VAT and VAT returns in practice, then you should become familiar with the contents of the VAT guide in order to be able to refer to it when necessary.

Example

If you wish to look up more information about the topics covered so far in this chapter, then Section 3 of the VAT guide has the following:

3 Introduction and liability to VAT

   3.1 Introduction to VAT

   3.2 What VAT is

   3.3 VAT rates

   3.4 Reduced-rated supplies

   3.5 Zero-rated supplies

   3.6 Exempt supplies

   3.7 Further information on liability and rates of VAT

6.4 VAT enquiries helpline

If a taxpayer cannot find the answer to their queries on the HMRC website, then a telephone helpline is available. When you call, you should have a note of your VAT registration number and postcode.

Taxpayers can also write to HMRC or ask HMRC online about VAT queries.

 Test your understanding 12

Which of the following is **NOT** a good source of information on VAT?

A   The HMRC website

B   A taxation magazine with a VAT section

C   A press release from a reputable accountancy firm about a recent change in VAT rules

D   A CPD course on direct taxation

7 Keeping up to date with VAT

7.1 Introduction

VAT changes regularly because of new legislation, and the precedent established by VAT case law.

It is important for everyone involved in VAT work to keep up to date, as failing to apply VAT rules correctly can cost the business money and may lead to penalties for incorrect returns or underpayments.

From an ethical point of view, it is important for AAT members and students to keep up to date in order that they may give competent advice.

Changes in VAT regulations normally take effect on a specified date and a business must ensure that they comply with the new rules from that date.

7.2 Ways of keeping up to date

Sources of information about VAT changes would include:

- the UK government website which has a VAT section (section 4.2)
- circulars from accountancy firms – most firms issue a newsletter to clients, which can often be accessed on their website
- specialist tax journals
- CPD courses
- networking meetings with fellow professionals.

7.3 Continuing professional development (CPD)

The AAT expects all full and fellow members to undertake continuing professional development (CPD) each year to ensure they are up-to-date and competent to do their work.

For a member involved in VAT work this would include being aware of any new rules and regulations.

7.4 Ethical considerations

AAT members and students are required to follow the AAT Code of Professional Ethics. These require that AAT members act with:

- integrity
- objectivity
- professional competence and due care
- confidentiality
- professional behaviour.

It is important to keep up to date with VAT legislation and any changes in order to act with professional competence and due care.

7.5 Impact on an organisation's recording systems

Legislative changes can have a significant impact on the recording systems of both HMRC and businesses with associated costs to be incurred to reflect the changes.

For example, when the rates of VAT change, supplies are reclassified, registration thresholds and/or registration rules change, significant costs can arise for a business.

Additional costs may include:

- staff training (and/or recruitment)
- adapting IT systems
- purchasing new software
- reprinting stationery, and
- additional time required for administrative (non-productive) work as opposed to profit-generating work.

More details on the impact of VAT rate changes on a business can be found in Chapter 3.

Test your understanding 13

Which one of the following is **NOT** a good reason to keep up to date with VAT?

A   It enables you to act with competence

B   Keeping up-to-date means that you are able to advise the business you work for and make it less likely to incur a penalty for a breach of the VAT rules

C   If you are up to date with the rules then it is easier to find ways around them and avoid paying over the VAT you have charged to customers

D   It may save the business money if it applies the rules correctly

8 Summary

This chapter has covered some important areas for VAT.

Dealing with VAT and discounts is an important area.

VAT invoices must include certain details and in normal circumstances must be given or sent to a VAT-registered purchaser. In practice, this means that all purchasers will be provided with a VAT invoice whether or not they are registered. However, retailers do not need to issue invoices unless a customer requests an invoice.

All businesses can issue less detailed invoices if the VAT-inclusive value of the supply is £250 or less.

Credit notes sent out by a business must include the same details as the invoice.

Pro-forma invoices must not include VAT.

It is also important to appreciate the cost implications of implementing new legislation and the significance and potential costs of mistakes made as a result of not being up to date.

If you need to find out more about VAT, then it is important to know where to look. The VAT guide (VAT Notice 700) and the HMRC website cover everything a typical business would need to know about VAT. Of course, you do not need to know all this material; you simply need to know where you might look to find it.

It is important for your professional competence to keep up to date on VAT. There are a number of ways in which you can find out the latest information about VAT.

Test your understanding answers

 Test your understanding 1

1   VAT on 6 metre hosepipes = £10.34 (£51.68 × 20% = £10.336)

2   VAT on bags of compost = £27.74 (£138.72 × 20% = £27.744)

3   VAT on kitchen units = £216.91 (£1,084.57 × 20% = £216.914)

All rounded mathematically to the nearest penny.

 Test your understanding 2

A   1
B   2
C   3
D   1
E   3

 Test your understanding 3

The correct answer is C.

The **VAT-inclusive** value of supplies on a simplified invoice cannot exceed £250.

Test your understanding 4

1   True – it is only compulsory to issue VAT invoices to registered traders.

2   False – the £250 limit is a VAT-inclusive amount.

3   True – VAT invoices form the evidence for the reclaim of input tax.

4   True

5   False – it includes VAT-inclusive amounts rather than VAT-exclusive amounts for each product.

Test your understanding 5

The correct answer is C.

	£ p
List price of goods	380.00
Less: 10% trade discount	(38.00)
Amount on which VAT to be calculated	342.00
VAT (20% × £342.00)	68.40

Alternative calculation:
VAT = (£380.00 × 90%) at 20%   68.40

Test your understanding 6

VAT must be charged on the price payable after discount.

£180.00 ((£1,000 – 10% of £1,000) = £900 × 20%)

£416.67 (£2,500 × 20/120) rounded to the nearest penny

£138.00 (£750 – 8% of £750) × 20%

Test your understanding 7

The correct answer is B.

The invoice will show £220 plus VAT of £44 (20% of £220)

The credit note will show discount of £4.40 (2% of £220) plus VAT of £0.88 (20% of £4.40)

This gives net VAT of £43.12 (£44 – £0.88)

VAT must be charged only on the standard-rated supplies. There is VAT of £0 on zero-rated items so they are ignored in this calculation.

Note that the VAT could have been calculated directly as:

£43.12 ((£220 – 2% of £220) × 20%), or
£43.12 (£220 × 98% × 20%)

 Test your understanding 8

The correct answer is B.

A sales credit note cancels out a sale thus reducing the sales, or outputs, of the business and consequently reducing the output VAT of the business.

 Test your understanding 9

The correct answer is D.

A purchase debit note cancels out a purchase thus reducing the purchases, or inputs, of the business and consequently reducing the input VAT of the business.

 Test your understanding 10

A and C are false.

A pro-forma invoice is NOT a valid tax invoice, nor is it evidence that allows the customer to reclaim input tax.

Test your understanding 11

Engineering Supplies Ltd

This invoice is a valid VAT invoice, which should be processed as a March input.

The input VAT of £533.46 can be reclaimed in the quarter to 31 March 2024.

Alpha Stationery

This is a valid simplified VAT invoice, which should also be processed as a March input.

The VAT of £2.47 (£14.84 × 20/120) can be reclaimed in the quarter to 31 March 2024.

Jamieson and Co

This is a pro-forma invoice so cannot be treated as a March input.

The VAT cannot be reclaimed until a valid VAT invoice is received.

 Test your understanding 12

The correct answer is D.

VAT is an indirect tax so a CPD course on direct taxation would not be a good source of information on VAT.

The other three options are all ways of finding information about VAT.

 Test your understanding 13

The correct answer is C.

AAT members and students are required to act with professional competence.

Avoiding paying VAT due to HMRC is in breach of professional competence and will lead to penalties (and possible criminal charges).

Input and output tax

Introduction

This chapter deals with some of the special rules for recovering input tax and charging output tax.

It also explains what happens when a business makes both taxable and exempt supplies and is therefore partly-exempt.

ASSESSMENT CRITERIA	CONTENTS
VAT Calculations (2.3)	1 Recovery of input tax 2 Output tax – capital assets 3 Partial exemption

1 Recovery of input tax

1.1 Conditions

Input VAT is usually recoverable by registered traders, on goods and services that are supplied to them. In order to recover the input tax, the following conditions must be met:

- the goods or services must be supplied for business purposes. Traders cannot recover input VAT on items bought for personal use.

- A VAT invoice is usually needed to support the claim.

- The input VAT must not be 'blocked' (i.e. irrecoverable).

Note that there is no distinction between revenue and capital expenditure for VAT.

Input VAT can be recovered on purchases of capital assets as well as revenue expenditure, provided the conditions above are satisfied.

1.2 Irrecoverable (blocked) input VAT

Input VAT on the following goods and services cannot be recovered:

- Most forms of business entertaining.

- Purchase of cars, unless they are 100% used for business purposes (e.g. car owned by a driving school purely used to give driving lessons, a taxi or a pool car used by employees).

  However, VAT can be recovered on the purchase of commercial vehicles like vans and lorries.

1.3 Business entertaining

In general, a business cannot recover input VAT on entertaining. However, there are some cases where VAT on entertaining **can** be recovered.

- Employee entertaining (e.g. staff parties, staff outings and team building events).

  If non-employees are included, the business can only recover input VAT on the proportion of the expenses that relate to:

  – employees, and

  – non-employees who are customers from overseas.

- VAT on entertaining overseas customers can be recovered.

Reference material

Information about VAT on vehicles and entertainment expenses can be found in the 'Blocked expenses and VAT' section of your reference material provided in the real assessment, so you do not need to learn it.

Why not look up the correct part of the reference material in the introduction to this text book now?

 Test your understanding 1

You are given the following information about business costs for the quarter to 31 December 2024.

Complete the table to show the amount of input tax that can be reclaimed on each item. State your answer rounded to the nearest penny.

All items are standard-rated for VAT purposes.

	Item	VAT-inclusive cost £	Input tax recoverable £
1	Car to be used by the managing director 60% for business and 40% privately	16,600.00	
2	Delivery van	17,500.00	
3	Staff party – staff were each allowed to bring a guest. Half the cost is estimated to be for these guests	630.00	
4	Entertaining UK customers and suppliers	526.00	
5	Car to be used as a pool car (i.e. available for all employees and kept at the business premises)	11,475.00	

Test your understanding 2

You are given the following information about purchases and expenses of a manufacturing business in the quarter to 30 June 2024.

Select Yes or No in the final column to show if the input tax on each item can be reclaimed.

Description	Input VAT £ p	Reclaim input VAT?
Car – for personal use by employee	1,960.00	Yes/No
Overseas customer entertainment	235.50	Yes/No
Staff party	142.70	Yes/No
Office supplies	27.45	Yes/No
Lorry	4,000.00	Yes/No

1.4 Motor expenses

Even though businesses cannot usually recover input VAT on the purchase cost of a car, a business can recover input VAT incurred on the running costs of a car such as fuel and repairs.

This applies even when there is some private use of the car.

When a business pays fuel costs for an employee or sole trader, and there is some private use of the vehicle, extra output tax will be payable.

This extra output tax is called a **fuel scale charge,** and varies with the CO_2 emissions of the car. The fuel scale charge is a **VAT-inclusive figure** so the VAT element is calculated as 1/6. However, the scale charge tables supplied by HMRC do this calculation for you.

Note that the scale charges are given in 5g/km intervals. If a car has an emission figure which is not exactly equal to one of the scale charges on the list, then it has to be rounded down to the next lower figure.

Example

Forge Ltd provides a company car to Charles and pays for all of his private fuel. The CO_2 emission level of the car is 204g/km.

The scale charge table shows (for a 3-month period):

200g/km	£ 526	VAT £87.67
205g/km	£ 544	VAT £90.67

What is the output VAT payable per quarter by Forge Ltd?

Solution

The scale figure for 200g/km is used, as 204g/km is rounded down to the nearest 5g/km.

The VAT-exclusive amount of £438.33 (£526 – £ 87.67) will be added to the total outputs on the company's VAT return (Chapter 6) and additional output tax of £87.67 will be payable by the company.

If a business does not want to pay a fuel scale charge, then it can either:

(a) reclaim only VAT on business fuel (detailed records of business and private mileage need to be kept to prove the business mileage), or

(b) not claim any VAT on fuel at all, even for commercial vehicles. This has the advantage of being simple and is useful if mileage is low.

 Reference material

Information about VAT on road fuel can be found in the 'Fuel scale charge and VAT' section of your reference material provided in the real assessment, so you do not need to learn it.

Why not look up the correct part of the reference material in the introduction to this text book now?

Test your understanding 3

Scott Ltd provides a car to an employee who uses it for both private and business use. All running expenses of the car are paid for by the company including fuel.

Which one of the following statements is true?

A   There are no VAT implications

B   The company can recover all of the input tax on the running costs and need take no further action

C   The company can recover all of the input tax on the running costs of the car and must add an amount to output tax determined by a scale charge

D   The company cannot recover input tax on running costs of the car but must add an amount to output tax determined by a scale charge

2   Output tax – capital assets

2.1   Introduction

Registered traders must charge output tax on all taxable supplies at the appropriate rate. This includes sales of capital assets as well as normal revenue sales.

2.2   Sales of capital assets

Normally when a registered trader sells a capital asset VAT will be charged at the standard rate on the sale price.

However, if the asset is a car on which the input tax was blocked (i.e. the trader could not recover the input tax on acquisition), then no output VAT is charged as it is an exempt sale.

If the input VAT was recoverable on the car, then output VAT is charged on the sale price as normal.

Test your understanding 4

You are given the following information about sales of capital assets in the quarter to 31 December 2024.

Complete the table to show the amount of output tax that must be charged on each item. State your answer rounded to the nearest penny.

Item	Input tax recovered	Sale proceeds (excl VAT) £	Output tax £
Van	Yes	11,000	
Car (1)	Yes	9,500	
Car (2)	No	10,550	
Machinery	Yes	21,000	

 Test your understanding 5

You are given the following information about sales of capital assets in the quarter to 31 December 2024.

Complete the table to show the amount of output tax that must be charged on each item. State your answer rounded to the nearest penny.

Item	Input tax recovered	Sale proceeds (excl VAT) £	Output tax £
Computer	Yes	2,100	
Car	No	10,000	
Van	Yes	12,500	
Motorcycle	Yes	6,760	

3 Partial exemption

3.1 Partial exemption

A taxable person who makes both taxable supplies and exempt supplies is referred to as a **partly-exempt** trader. For this purpose, it does not matter if the taxable supplies are standard or zero-rated.

The problem with partial exemption is that taxable supplies entitle the supplier to a credit for input tax in respect of related costs, whereas exempt supplies do not.

3.2 The standard method

If the input tax relating to exempt supplies is classed as de minimis (low), HMRC will allow the business to reclaim the input tax even though it relates to making exempt supplies.

The most common method used is to divide input tax into three parts:

- Relating wholly to taxable supplies – all recoverable

- Relating wholly to exempt supplies – irrecoverable

- Relating to overheads – proportion which relate to taxable supplies can be recovered, leaving the rest irrecoverable

The standard method calculates the proportion relating to taxable supplies using the following formula:

$$\text{Unallocated VAT on overheads} \times \frac{\text{Value of taxable supplies in the period (excluding VAT)}}{\text{Total value of supplies in the period (excluding VAT)}} = \text{Recoverable percentage of residual input VAT*}$$

*The percentage is rounded up to the next whole number.

The total irrecoverable input VAT then comprises that relating wholly to exempt supplies and the balance of the unallocated VAT.

If the total irrecoverable input tax does not exceed 50% of the total input VAT **and** is no more than £625 per month on average, then all of the input VAT can be recovered.

This calculation is initially completed on a quarterly basis however there is an overall adjustment at the end of the VAT year such that the final determination is based on the annual figures. This helps smooth out any seasonal variations that may distort the calculations.

Example

Julie's business makes both taxable and exempt supplies

In her latest VAT period, quarter ended 30 June 2024, input tax of £15,000 was analysed as follows:

Activity	Input VAT
Taxable supplies (£92,000)	£12,000
Exempt supplies (£10,000)	£1,000
Overheads	£2,000

Standard Method

The input VAT must be analysed and split between the taxable and exempt parts of the business.

The input VAT **relating to taxable supplies** is calculated as follows:

Input VAT attributable to taxable supplies

1) **Directly attributable** input VAT of £12,000, this is recoverable.

2) Proportion of unallocated VAT **(Overheads)**:

Taxable supplies ÷ Total supplies

£92,000 ÷ (£92,000 + £10,000) = 90.1% (Round up to 91%)

VAT on overheads = £2,000 × 91% = £1,820 this is also recoverable

Then calculate the VAT that **relates to exempt supplies**

1) **Directly attributable** input VAT of £1,000

2) Proportion of unallocated VAT **(Overheads)**:

£2,000 - £1,820 = £180

Calculate the monthly average of input tax relating to exempt supplies:

(£1,000 + £180) ÷ 3 = £393

This is less than £625 per month on average

AND

The input VAT relating to exempt supplies is less than 50% of the total input VAT (£1,180 is less than 50% × £15,000 = £7,500)

Therefore, ALL £15,000 of input VAT can be recovered.

Reference material

Information about partial exemption can be found in the 'Partial exemption for VAT' section of your reference material provided in the real assessment, so you do not need to learn it.

Why not look up the correct part of the reference material in the introduction to this text book now?

Test your understanding 6

A business supplies goods that are a mixture of standard-rated and exempt. Which one of the following statements is true?

A   All of the input VAT can be reclaimed

B   None of the input VAT can be reclaimed

C   All of the input VAT can be reclaimed provided certain de minimis conditions are met

D   Only the input VAT on goods and services purchased for use in making standard-rated supplies can ever be reclaimed

4 Summary

This chapter has looked at the rules for recovering input tax and examined the items that have a restricted recovery.

Cars with some private use and business entertaining are the examples of 'blocked' input tax that you are required to know for your assessment. There are some exceptions for entertaining.

The treatment of motor expenses is also an important area and you should be aware of the different treatments possible.

Finally, the chapter deals with the topic of partly-exempt businesses. Such businesses may have to restrict the amount of input tax they can recover.

Test your understanding answers

Test your understanding 1

1   None – the car is not used 100% for business

2   £2,916.67 (£17,500.00 × 1/6) (round to the nearest penny)

3   £52.50 (£630.00 ÷ 2 × 1/6) VAT is recoverable on half the cost

4   None – blocked VAT

5   £1,912.50 (£11,475.00 × 1/6) – car is used 100% for business

Test your understanding 2

Car – No, input tax not recoverable if there is any private use of the car

Overseas customer entertainment – Yes, input tax is recoverable

Staff party – Yes, input tax is recoverable

Office supplies – Yes, input tax is recoverable

Lorry – Yes, input tax is recoverable on commercial vehicles

Test your understanding 3

The correct answer is C.

When a business supplies a car to an employee who uses the car at least partly privately, and pays for fuel, then the business can recover the input VAT on running costs including the fuel.

However, the company must account for output tax determined by a table of scale charges.

Test your understanding 4

Van	£2,200.00 (£11,000 × 20%)
Car 1	£1,900.00 (£9,500 × 20%)
Car 2	Nil – this is an exempt supply because the business was not able to recover the input tax on the purchase.
Machinery	£4,200.00 (£21,000 × 20%)

 Test your understanding 5

Computer	£420.00 (£2,100 × 20%)
Car	Nil – sale of a car on which the input tax was not recoverable is an exempt supply.
Van	£2,500.00 (£12,500 × 20%)
Motorcycle	£1,352.00 (£6,760 × 20%)

 Test your understanding 6

The correct answer is C.

A partly-exempt business has to apportion input tax in proportion to the levels of taxable and exempt supplies.

However, if the exempt input tax is below the de minimis amount the whole of the input tax can be recovered.

VAT accounting schemes

5

Introduction

This chapter deals with VAT accounting. There are several special schemes available for small businesses. These schemes have a number of advantages. They can reduce administration (annual accounting and flat rate scheme) or improve cash flow (cash accounting).

You should pay particular attention to which businesses are eligible and the reasons why a business might join one of these schemes.

ASSESSMENT CRITERIA
VAT registration and deregistration requirements (1.2)
Special schemes (1.4)
Communicating information on VAT related matters (5.1)

CONTENTS

1   Standard scheme
2   Annual accounting
3   Cash accounting
4   The flat rate scheme

1 Standard scheme

1.1 Return periods

When a business is first registered, it automatically joins the standard VAT scheme. If the business wishes to make use of any of the special accounting schemes described in this chapter, then it must apply to do so.

In the standard scheme, all registered traders have to submit a VAT return for every return period. Information to complete the return is taken from sales and purchase information – usually from the VAT control account compiled from the original and verified daybook totals. Any amounts of VAT due must be paid over to HMRC, or a claim made for VAT to be reimbursed.

Return periods are usually for 3 months.

1.2 Submission of returns

All traders must submit their returns online, and pay their VAT electronically.

Returns must be submitted to HMRC within **one month and seven days after the end of the return period.**

Completion of VAT returns is explained and illustrated in Chapter 6.

1.3 Making Tax Digital (MTD)

VAT registered businesses are automatically required to use MTD, i.e. they have to keep their VAT records digitally and provide their VAT return information to HMRC through MTD-compatible software.

HMRC will sign up all new VAT registered business to MTD for VAT automatically, unless they are exempt.

A limited number of businesses are exempt from the MTD rules. These are businesses that HMRC is satisfied one of the following applies to:

- It is not practicable for the business to use MTD because of age, disability, remote location or some other valid reason, or

- The business is subject to insolvency proceedings, or

- The business is entirely run by people whose religious beliefs do not allow for the use of electronic communications or software.

Businesses must continue under MTD even if taxable turnover falls below the registration threshold in the future. This obligation does not apply if the business deregisters for VAT.

The exchange of information with HMRC needs to be via an Application Programming Interface (API) and it is generally expected that API-enabled software will also be the method used for data retention, although other bridging software or API-enabled spreadsheets could be used as an alternative. Details of MTD-compatible third party software are available on HMRC's website.

An accountancy firm can register as an agent for MTD and then submit returns on client's behalf. In this scenario the agent would ensure that MTD-compatible software has been used when submitting client's VAT returns. The responsibility for correct submission does however still remain with the tax payer.

1.4 Payment of VAT

If a VAT payment is due, it must be paid electronically. The latest payment date is the same as the due date for the VAT return, that is **one month and seven days after the end of the return period**.

The extra seven days does not apply:

- if the trader uses the annual accounting scheme (section 2)

- if the trader has to make monthly payments (compulsory for large businesses).

If a trader pays by direct debit the payment is taken by HMRC from the trader's account three working days after the normal return submission date, or three days after the return is actually submitted if this is later.

 Example

Jonas has a quarterly return period to 30 April 2024.

He must submit the return and settle any liability electronically by 7 June 2024.

If he pays by direct debit, Jonas' payment will be made on 12 June 2024. This is three working days after the normal submission date.

Other electronic payment methods include:

- By debit or credit card over the internet
- Bank transfer
- Faster payment using an online bank account

 Test your understanding 1

Oak Ltd has prepared its VAT return for the quarter ended 30 September 2024.

1   When is Oak Ltd's return due?

   A   14 October 2024

   B   31 October 2024

   C   6 November 2024

   D   7 November 2024

2   Assuming Oak Ltd submits the return on time, and pays by direct debit, when will HMRC take the money from Oak Ltd's bank account?

   A   The same date as the return is due

   B   3 days after the return is due

   C   3 working days after the return is due

1.5   Refunds of VAT

If the business has more input tax than output tax in a particular VAT period, then it will be due a refund.

Before making a repayment, HMRC makes additional checks on the return to ensure the claim is valid.

Provided the additional checks confirm a repayment is due, the repayment is automatically made directly into the trader's bank account.

In most cases, this will be within 30 days of receiving the return. If HMRC is late in refunding the VAT owed the trader may be entitled to repayment interest. Repayment interest is in Chapter 7.

Traders who regularly receive repayments can choose to submit monthly returns.

A refund will not be made automatically if there is an outstanding debt due to HMRC.

1.6   Other schemes

There are a number of special schemes for accounting for VAT. These are designed to help small businesses by reducing administration and may improve cash flow.

The schemes that you must know about are:

- annual accounting
- cash accounting
- flat rate scheme.

Note that all of the schemes are optional to join and are subject to conditions.

There are also special schemes for retailers and businesses that sell second-hand goods. However, you do not need to know details of these.

2   Annual accounting

2.1   Purpose of the scheme

Smaller businesses may find it costly or inconvenient to prepare the standard four quarterly VAT returns.

An annual accounting scheme allows a business to submit a single VAT return for a 12-month period (normally the accounting period of the business). This helps relieve the burden of administration.

2.2   How the scheme works

Only one VAT return is submitted each year, but VAT payments must still be made regularly.

The scheme works as follows:

1   The annual return must be filed within **2 months** of the end of the annual return period.

2   Payments on account are made during the year. The trader can either make monthly or quarterly payments on account.

- Under the monthly scheme, nine payments on account are made at the end of months 4 to 12 of the year. Each payment represents 10% of the VAT liability for the previous year.

- Under the quarterly scheme, three payments on account are made at the end of months 4, 7 and 10. Each payment is calculated as 25% of the VAT liability of the prior year.

- A new business will base its payments on an estimate of the VAT liability for the year.

3 A balancing payment or repayment is made when the annual return is submitted.

4 All payments must be made electronically with **no 7-day extension**.

5 Additional payments can be made by the business when desired.

2.3 Conditions for the annual accounting scheme

The scheme is aimed at smaller businesses and it is optional to join, however conditions need to be satisfied to be eligible to join.

- Businesses can join the scheme, provided its taxable turnover (excluding VAT and the sale of capital assets) in the next 12 months is expected to be no more than £1,350,000.

- The business must be up-to-date with its VAT returns. However, a business does not need a history of VAT returns to join. It can join the scheme from the day it registers.

- Businesses must leave the scheme if its estimated taxable turnover (excluding VAT) for the next 12 months is more than £1,600,000.

  If a business takes over another business as a going concern, the estimated taxable turnover (excluding VAT) of the new combined business for the next 12 months must be assessed and compared to the £1,600,000 threshold, to decide whether the business should immediately leave the scheme.

2.4 Who might use the scheme?

The scheme is useful to businesses that want to:

- reduce administration because only one VAT return is needed instead of four, and businesses have two months to prepare the return instead of the usual one month

- fix its VAT payments in advance, at least for its nine monthly payments. This is useful for budgeting cash flow.

It is not useful if:

- the business receives repayments as only one repayment per year will be received.

- the taxable turnover of the business is decreasing, as then the interim payments might be higher than under the standard scheme and the business will have to wait until submission of the annual VAT return to receive any repayment due.

Test your understanding 2

Jump Ltd applies to use the annual accounting scheme from 1 January 2024, making monthly payments on account. The company's VAT liability for the year ended 31 December 2024 was £3,600.00. The actual VAT liability for the year ended 31 December 2024 is £3,820.00.

1 When must Jump Ltd's VAT return be filed?

   A   31 January 2025

   B   28 February 2025

   C   31 March 2025

2 Which ONE of the following statements about Jump Ltd's payment of VAT during the year ended 31 December 2024 is true?

   A   Jump Ltd must make nine monthly payments of £360.00

   B   Jump Ltd must make nine monthly payments of £382.00

   C   Jump Ltd must make twelve monthly payments of £300.00

   D   Jump Ltd must make twelve monthly payments of £318.33

3 What is the balancing payment/repayment due from/to Jump Ltd when its VAT return for the year ended 31 December 2024 is filed?

The annual accounting scheme can be used in conjunction either with the cash accounting scheme or with the flat rate scheme, but not both schemes.

 Test your understanding 3

A VAT registered business has a year ended 30 June 2024 and uses the annual accounting scheme, making monthly payments.

1 Which one of the following statements is true?

   A   The whole VAT liability for the year is payable on 30 June 2024

   B   The whole VAT liability for the year is payable on 31 August 2024

   C   The VAT liability is payable in nine monthly instalments starting on 31 October 2023 with a balancing payment on 31 July 2024

> D   The VAT liability is payable in nine monthly instalments starting on 31 October 2023 with a balancing payment on 31 August 2024
>
> 2   The annual VAT return is due to be submitted by which date?
>
> A   31 July 2024
>
> B   31 August 2024

 Reference material

Information about annual accounting can be found in the 'Special accounting schemes for VAT' section of your reference material provided in the real assessment, so you do not need to learn it.

Why not look up the correct part of the reference material in the introduction to this text book now?

3   Cash accounting

3.1   How the scheme works

Usually VAT is accounted for based on invoices issued and received in a return period. Accordingly:

- Output VAT is paid to HMRC by reference to the period in which the tax point occurs (usually the time of delivery or invoice date), regardless of whether payment has been received from the customer.

- Input VAT is reclaimed from HMRC by reference to the invoices received in the return period, even if payment has not been made to the supplier.

However, under the cash accounting scheme a business accounts for VAT based on when payment is actually received from customers or made to suppliers. The tax point becomes the date of receipt or payment.

Under the cash accounting scheme, invoices will still be sent to customers and received from suppliers in the normal way, but the key record that must be kept is a cash book. This should summarise all the payments made and received, and have a **separate column for VAT**.

3.2 Conditions

As with annual accounting, the scheme is aimed at smaller businesses, it is optional to join and conditions need to be satisfied to be eligible to join.

- The trader's VAT returns must be up-to-date and no convictions for VAT offences must have been made in the last 12 months, for example VAT evasion.

- Estimated taxable turnover, excluding VAT and sales of capital assets, must not exceed £1,350,000 for the next year.

- Once in the scheme, a trader must leave once their annual taxable turnover, excluding VAT, exceeds £1,600,000.

  If a business takes over another business as a going concern, the estimated taxable turnover (excluding VAT) of the new combined business must be assessed and compared to the £1,600,000 threshold to decide whether the business should immediately leave the scheme.

- When a business leaves the scheme, it must account for all outstanding VAT (i.e. on amounts receivable less amounts payable), as it will be moving to a system where VAT is accounted for on invoices not on a cash basis.

3.3 Advantages and disadvantages

Advantages	Disadvantages
• Businesses selling on credit do not have to pay output VAT to HMRC until it receives cash from customers.	• Input tax cannot be claimed until the invoice is paid. This delays recovery of input VAT.
• This gives automatic relief for bad debts (i.e. irrecoverable debts) because if the customer does not pay, then the VAT on the invoice due does not have to be paid to HMRC. Cash flow is improved.	• Not suitable for businesses with a lot of cash sales or zero-rated supplies. • Using cash accounting in these situations causes a delay in the recovery of input VAT, with no associated benefit relating to output VAT.
• Cash accounting can be used together with annual accounting (but not the flat rate scheme).	• If a business uses cash accounting as soon as it registers, it will be unable to reclaim VAT on its stock (i.e. inventory) and assets until the invoices for these items are paid.

Test your understanding 4

Would each of the following businesses benefit from joining the cash accounting scheme? Select Yes or No for each business. ·

1   JB Ltd, which operates a retail shop selling directly to the public. All sales are for cash and all purchases are made on credit. JB Ltd's supplies are all standard-rated.   YES/NO

2   Amber and Co, which manufactures and sells computer printers to other businesses. This is a standard-rated business and all sales and purchases are made on credit.   YES/NO

3   John Smith, a sole trader who manufactures children's shoes and sells them to retailers. This is a zero-rated activity and all sales and purchases are made on credit.   YES/NO

 Test your understanding 5

Indicate whether the following statements about the cash accounting scheme are true or false.

Tick one box on each line.

		True	False
1	VAT invoices are not issued to customers		
2	The scheme gives automatic bad debt relief		
3	Cash accounting is useful for businesses with a high proportion of cash sales		
4	If a business adopts cash accounting then customers cannot reclaim input VAT until they pay their invoices		
5	A business cannot join the cash accounting scheme if their VAT returns are not up-to-date		

Reference material

Information about cash accounting can be found in the 'Special accounting schemes for VAT' section of your reference material provided in the real assessment, so you do not need to learn it.

Why not look up the correct part of the reference material in the introduction to this text book now?

4 The flat rate scheme

4.1 Purpose of the scheme

The aim of the flat rate scheme is to simplify the way in which very small businesses calculate their VAT liability.

4.2 How the scheme works

Under the flat rate scheme, a business calculates its VAT liability by simply **applying a flat rate percentage to its total VAT-inclusive turnover**.

This removes the need to calculate and record detailed output and input VAT information. In some cases, it can save the business money.

- The flat rate percentage is applied to the gross (VAT-inclusive) **total turnover** figure.

    This includes standard-rated, zero-rated and exempt supplies.

    No input VAT is recovered.

- The percentage varies according to the type of trade in which the business is involved.

    If a business joins the flat rate scheme during its first year of VAT registration, it will receive a 1% discount on the normal percentage relevant for its trade or industry sector.

    Note that if you need to use an appropriate percentage in the assessment, it will be given to you.

- If the business changes business sector it must change flat rate percentage to the one appropriate for the new sector.

- The flat rate scheme is **only** used to calculate the VAT due to HMRC.

In other respects, VAT is dealt with in the normal way:

- A **VAT invoice** must still be issued to customers and VAT charged at the appropriate rate, for example 20% for a standard rated supply.

- A **VAT control account** must still be maintained.

- It is not possible to join both the flat rate scheme and the cash accounting scheme. However, the flat rate scheme can be used in conjunction with the annual accounting scheme.

4.3 Conditions for the scheme

The scheme is optional. However, in order to join the scheme, the **taxable** turnover of the business (excluding VAT), for the next 12 months, must not be expected to exceed £150,000.

Once in the scheme, a business can stay in until its **total VAT-inclusive** income (i.e. all turnover **including taxable and exempt supplies**) for the previous 12 months exceeds £230,000, or it is expected to exceed this in the next 12 months.

If a business takes over another business as a going concern, the total VAT-inclusive turnover (taxable and exempt) of the new combined business for the previous 12 months must be assessed and compared to the £230,000 threshold to decide whether the business should leave the scheme.

 Example

Simon runs a business selling computer supplies. He registered for VAT and joined the flat rate scheme a few years ago.

If the flat rate percentage for this type of business is 12%, how much VAT should Simon pay to HMRC for the quarter ended 30 June 2023 when his turnover (including VAT) is £39,000?

Solution

£4,680.00 (£39,000 × 12%)

4.4 Advantages and disadvantages of the flat rate scheme

The advantages of the scheme include the following:

- A business does not have to record the VAT incurred on each individual purchase.

- Easier administration as the business does not have to decide which amounts of input VAT can be reclaimed and which cannot.

- The business gets a discount of 1% if it joins this scheme in its first year of VAT registration.

- The business may pay less VAT than using the normal method.

- The business has certainty as the percentage of turnover that has to be paid to HMRC, as VAT is known in advance.

- There is less chance of making a mistake in calculating VAT.

The percentage used in flat rate accounting is fixed for particular trade sectors and takes into account the mix of standard-rated, zero-rated and exempt sales made by the average business in that sector.

The scheme may not be suitable for businesses that do not have the same mix as an average business.

In particular, it would not be suitable for:

- businesses that regularly receive repayments under normal VAT accounting

- businesses that buy a higher proportion of standard-rated items than others in its trade sector do, as it would not be able to reclaim the input VAT on these purchases

- businesses that make a higher proportion of zero-rated or exempt sales than others in its trade do.

4.5 Limited cost businesses

If a business qualifies as a limited cost business, then VAT will be calculated under the flat rate scheme using 16.5% rather than the percentage based on the particular business sector.

This removes one of the main advantages of the flat rate scheme and some businesses may actually pay more VAT than they would under the standard VAT system.

A business is classed as a limited cost business if its VAT-inclusive expenditure on goods is less than either:

- 2% of its VAT-inclusive turnover

- £1,000 a year (if its costs are more than 2% of VAT-inclusive turnover).

Goods, for the purposes of a limited cost business, must be used exclusively for business purposes and exclude the following:

- capital expenditure

- food or drink for consumption by the flat-rate business or its employees

- vehicles, vehicle parts and fuel (except where the business provides transport services, for example, a taxi business).

 Example

Claire runs a wedding photography business and uses the flat rate scheme to prepare her VAT returns.

Claire's VAT-inclusive turnover for the quarter ended 30 September 2024 is £14,400. Her VAT-inclusive cost of goods for this period was £275.

If the flat rate percentage for this type of business is 11%, how much VAT should Claire pay over for the quarter ended 30 September 2024?

Solution

Although the cost of Claire's goods comes to more than £250 (the quarterly equivalent of £1,000), they amount to less than 2% of her VAT inclusive turnover (2% × £14,400 = £288) and therefore she is a limited cost trader.

As a result, her VAT should be calculated using a percentage of 16.5% rather than the relevant percentage for her business type.

£2,376 (£14,400 × 16.5%)

4.6 Reclaiming VAT on capital expenditure

If a business that qualifies for the flat rate scheme spends in excess of £2,000 on a capital item (VAT-inclusive) then the business can specifically recover the input VAT on that item and this falls outside the flat rate scheme.

This means the input VAT will be recovered by adding it to Box 4 of the VAT return (Chapter 6).

Test your understanding 6

In the year ended 31 December 2024, Apple Ltd has annual sales to the general public of £100,000, all of which are standard-rated.

The company incurs standard-rated expenses of £4,500 per annum.

These figures include VAT.

1   What is Apple Ltd's VAT liability using the normal method?

    A   £19,100.00

    B   £15,916.67

    C   £20,000.00

    D   £16,666.67

2   What is Apple Ltd's VAT liability using the flat rate method assuming a percentage of 9%?

    A   £20,000.00

    B   £16,666.67

    C   £9,000.00

    D   £8,595.00

 Test your understanding 7

Indicate whether the following statements about the flat rate scheme are true or false.

Tick one box on each line.

		True	False
1	VAT invoices are not issued to customers.		
2	A VAT account need not be kept.		
3	Traders using the flat rate scheme can also join the annual accounting scheme.		

4	Traders can join the flat rate scheme if their taxable turnover for the last 12 months is below £230,000.		
5	The flat rate scheme percentage varies according to the trade sector of the business.		

 Test your understanding 8

Which one of the following is not an advantage of the flat rate scheme?

A   The business gets a discount of 1% on the flat rate percentage in the first year of registration.

B   VAT returns do not need to be completed.

C   The business does not have to record the VAT incurred on individual purchases.

D   The business has easier administration as it does not have to decide which input VAT can be reclaimed and which cannot.

 Test your understanding 9

In the year ended 31 December 2024, Pear Ltd has annual sales of £87,000, all of which are standard-rated and to the general public.

The company incurs standard-rated expenses of £6,100 per annum.

These figures are VAT-exclusive.

1   Select which of the following gives Pear Ltd's liability using the normal method.

    A   £13,483.33

    B   £17,400.00

    C   £16,180.00

    D   £14,500.00

2   Select which of the following gives Pear Ltd's VAT liability using the flat rate method, assuming a percentage of 8%.

    A   £6,960.00

    B   £8,352.00

Reference material

Information about the flat rate scheme can be found in the 'Special accounting schemes for VAT' section of your reference material provided in the real assessment, so you do not need to learn it.

Why not look up the correct part of the reference material in the introduction to this text book now?

 Test your understanding 10

1   Which one of the following statements is true?

   A   Traders using the normal accounting scheme usually submit their VAT returns every quarter

   B   Electronic VAT returns must be submitted 7 days after the end of the return period

   C   A trader is always permitted to pay VAT by sending a cheque through the post

2   What is the annual turnover threshold for eligibility to join the annual accounting scheme?

   A   £1,350,000

   B   £1,600,000

3   Is the following statement true or false?

   The cash accounting scheme can be used at the same time as the annual accounting scheme   TRUE/FALSE

4   John's VAT liability for the previous year was £7,200.00. He estimates it will be £7,800.00 this year. He joins the annual accounting scheme, making monthly payments

   What is the size of each instalment?

   A   £720.00

   B   £780.00

   C   £800.00

   D   £866.67

5   Which one of the following statements about cash accounting is false?

    A   Cash accounting is a disadvantage for a business selling zero-rated supplies

    B   VAT invoices need not be sent out

    C   The key record for determining VAT due is the cash book

6   Zak is a registered trader using the flat rate scheme with a percentage of 12%. His sales for the quarter are all standard-rated and are £75,000 inclusive of VAT. His business is not a limited cost business.

    What VAT should he pay to HMRC for the quarter?

    A   £9,000.00

    B   £7,500.00

7   Trystan owns a business with an annual taxable turnover of £800,000 and uses the annual accounting scheme.

    He transfers the business as a going concern to William and Sons, which has an existing taxable turnover of £900,000 and uses the annual accounting scheme.

    Trystan is employed by William and Sons as the manager to run his former business.

    Which of the following statements is true?

    A   Trystan's part of the business can continue to use the annual accounting scheme until its turnover exceeds £1,600,000.

    B   Trystan's part of the business can continue to use the annual accounting scheme for the next 12 months.

    C   As the turnover of the combined business exceeds £1,600,000 the whole combined business is no longer eligible to be in the annual accounting scheme.

5 Summary

Clearly, it is important for businesses to know when they are required to complete VAT returns and pay VAT to HMRC. The usual pattern is to complete returns and pay VAT either quarterly or monthly. This is the case unless the business has chosen annual accounting, which is one of the special schemes aimed at smaller businesses.

Annual accounting gives the advantages of only one annual VAT return and fixed regular VAT payments. The turnover thresholds for the scheme are the same as for cash accounting.

Cash accounting changes the normal tax point rules and allows the business to pay VAT to HMRC when it actually receives the cash from its customers rather than the delivery or invoice date. This gives automatic relief for bad debts (i.e. irrecoverable debts) but has the disadvantage that input VAT can only be claimed when suppliers are paid.

The flat rate scheme is aimed at simplifying VAT accounting for the very small business. The amount of VAT payable is determined by simply applying a fixed percentage to the VAT-inclusive turnover of the business. However, it is important to remember that the business still has to comply with the rules about issuing tax invoices.

Test your understanding answers

Test your understanding 1

1   The correct answer is D.

     7 November 2024 – one month and 7 days after the end of the VAT quarter.

2   The correct answer is C.

     Direct debit payments are taken from the trader's bank account 3 working days after the return is due.

Test your understanding 2

1   The correct answer is B.

     28 February 2025 = 2 months after the year-end.

2   The correct answer is A.

     Nine monthly payments must be made, each of which are 10% of the VAT liability for the previous year.

3   The balancing payment will be £580.00

     (£3,820.00 – (£360.00 × 9))

Test your understanding 3

1   The correct answer is D.

     This is how the annual accounting scheme payments are made.

2   The correct answer is B.

     31 August 2024 – two months after the year end.

Test your understanding 4

1   NO.   As sales are all in cash, the adoption of the cash accounting scheme would not affect the time when output VAT would be accounted for.

    However, the recovery of input VAT would be delayed until the business had paid its suppliers.

2   YES.   The business would benefit because it would only account for output VAT when the customer paid.

    Even though the recovery of input VAT would be delayed until the suppliers were paid, the amount of input VAT is likely to be less than output VAT so the business does gain a net cash flow advantage.

3   NO.   As the sales are zero-rated no output tax is payable. The adoption of the cash accounting scheme would simply delay the recovery of input VAT until the suppliers were paid.

 Test your understanding 5

1   False – VAT invoices must still be issued.

2   True – this is one of the advantages of the scheme.

3   False – businesses with a high level of cash sales do not benefit from cash accounting.

4   False – cash accounting does not affect customers.

5   True – this is one of the conditions for joining the scheme.

 Test your understanding 6

1   The correct answer is B.

    £15,916.67 (20/120 × (£100,000 – £4,500))

2   The correct answer is C.

    £9,000.00 (9% × £100,000)

Test your understanding 7

1   False – VAT invoices must still be supplied to customers.

2   False – A VAT account must still be kept.

3   True – It is possible to be in the flat rate and the annual accounting scheme.

4   False – the threshold to join the scheme is £150,000.

5   True – The flat rate percentage is determined by your trade sector.

 Test your understanding 8

The correct answer is B.

VAT returns must still be completed.

 Test your understanding 9

1   The correct answer is C.

(£87,000 – £6,100) × 20% = £16,180.00

2   The correct answer is B.

(£87,000 + 20% of £87,000) × 8% = £8,352.00

The percentage must be applied to the VAT-inclusive figure.

117

Test your understanding 10

1   The correct answer is A.

B is false as the time limit is 1 month and 7 days after the end of the return period.

C is false, as traders cannot pay by post.

2   The correct answer is A.

3   The statement is true.

4   The correct answer is A. (£7,200 ÷ 10) = £720.00

5   The correct answer is B.

6   The correct answer is A. (£75,000 × 12%) = £9,000.00.

7   The correct answer is C.

VAT returns and overseas aspects

Introduction

In this chapter we are going to look at the information that is contained in a VAT return. You are not required to complete a VAT return in your assessment, however, you are required to verify the information contained within a VAT return, and know what is contained within the majority of the boxes on the VAT return.

Businesses produce VAT returns digitally under MTD. This can be produced directly from the MTD-compatible accounting software that the business uses.

The extracted information is shown in a digitally produced VAT return (VAT 100 form). The business must then confirm that the information contained on the digital form is correct, and then submit the return digitally to HMRC. This summarises the transactions of a business for the relevant period.

This chapter also considers the VAT implications of trading overseas.

ASSESSMENT CRITERIA	CONTENTS
Extract relevant data from the accounting records (2.1)	1 The VAT return
VAT invoices (2.2)	2 Completing the VAT return
VAT calculations (2.3)	3 Overseas aspects of VAT
Make adjustments for errors & omissions in VAT returns (3.1)	
Verify information contained within VAT returns (3.2)	
Legislation, regulation, guidance and codes of practice (5.2)	

1 The VAT return

1.1 Introduction

The tax period for VAT is **three months**, or one month for taxpayers who choose to make monthly returns (usually taxpayers who receive regular refunds).

Under MTD the return is generated electronically from the accounting system or MTD-compatible bridging software that extracts the relevant details from other electronic records, for example a spreadsheet based accounting system. The taxpayer confirms that the information on the VAT return is correct and then digitally submits the VAT return to HMRC. A confirmation message is generated if the submission is successful.

The return summarises all the transactions for the period.

1.2 Timing of the VAT return

The taxpayer must submit the return within one month and seven days from the end of the tax period. The taxable person must ensure that the amount due (i.e. output tax collected less input tax deducted) clears in the HMRC bank account at the same time, unless a direct debit payment arrangement exists.

For more detail on VAT returns and payments, refer back to Chapter 5.

If a VAT repayment is due from HMRC, the VAT return must still be completed and submitted to the same time deadlines in order to be able to reclaim the amount due.

1.3 What a VAT return looks like

The online VAT return comprises nine boxes of information. The information shows the output and input VAT, overall VAT liability (or repayment due) together with information about sales and purchases.

Once the electronic submission has been successfully completed, the taxpayer can print a copy VAT return for their records.

An example of a copy VAT return is shown on the next page.

1.4 VAT return

Printed copy of VAT return for your records			
THIS IS FOR YOUR RECORDS ONLY. DO NOT SEND THIS TO HM Revenue and Customs.			
XYZ LTD	Registration Number: 123 4567 89		
	For the period:		
	01 Jan 2024 to 31 March 2024		
	Return Due Date: 07 May 2024		
	Date printed: 07 May 2024		
1	VAT due in the period on sales and other outputs	£	53,470.50
2	VAT due in the period on acquisitions of goods made in Northern Ireland from EU Member States	£	0
3	Total VAT due	£	53,470.50
4	VAT reclaimed in the period on the purchases and other inputs (including acquisitions in Northern Ireland from EU member states)	£	17,495.25
5	Net VAT to be paid to HMRC or reclaimed	£	35,975.25
6	Total value of sales and all other outputs excluding any VAT	£	273,590.00
7	Total value of purchases and all other inputs excluding any VAT	£	93,454.00
8	Total value of dispatches of goods and related costs (excluding VAT) from Northern Ireland to EU Member States	£	0
9	Total value of acquisitions of goods and related costs (excluding VAT) made in Northern Ireland from EU Member States	£	0
RETURN SUCCESSFULLY SUBMITTED: 07 May 2024			

Businesses will not complete the actual VAT return because returns are completed using MTD, with MTD-compatible software extracting the correct information digitally from business records. Businesses may however complete a draft return in advance to assist with their cashflow management.

There are nine boxes to complete with the relevant figures.

- Boxes 1 to 5 are actual VAT amounts and these should be completed in pounds and pence.

  Boxes 3 and 5 are subtotals, so a business only needs information for the remaining seven boxes if preparing a draft VAT return.

- Boxes 6 to 9 are totals of inputs and outputs and should be completed to the nearest whole pounds.

Boxes 2, 8 and 9 are for supplies of goods between European Union Member States involving Northern Ireland.

You are not required to have knowledge of these transactions, as they are not examinable.

2 Completing the VAT return

2.1 The VAT control account

The main source of information for the VAT return is the VAT control account.

The VAT control account is a record that must be maintained by the trader to show the amount of VAT that is due to or from HMRC at the end of each quarter. It provides the link between the VAT return entries and the underlying business records.

It is important that the figures on the VAT return are extracted correctly from the business records. Using MTD-compatible software ensures that this is the case. Typically, the information is extracted from the VAT control account.

The VAT control account is a nominal ledger account completed as part of double entry bookkeeping. The nominal ledger, as you should know from previous studies, is derived from business records such as the sales daybook, purchase daybook, cash book and from any adjustments made and reflected as journals.

The rationale behind MTD is that there are less errors when the VAT return is completed as this is now done electronically.

Entries in these ledgers must be made with integrity and with knowledge of the requirements of VAT records and regulation of VAT administration.

The use of a company's audited accounting records will satisfy the integrity of the information.

If a statutory audit of the business is not required, it should nonetheless make its own internal checks to ensure that the information extracted from the records and taken to the VAT control account is accurate and complete.

2.2 Differences between the VAT return and the accounting records

It is also important to realise that the balance on the VAT control account should agree to the balance of VAT payable/reclaimable on the VAT return.

In the assessment, you may be asked to select reasons why the VAT return is not correct or why there is a difference between the accounting records and the VAT return.

Possible reasons for the underlying records and the VAT return not reconciling include the following:

Incorrect transfer of data

If a business uses bridging software to submit VAT returns it is possible that an error is made when transferring data from any manual records into an electronic format. The MTD-compatible software extracts information from the electronic data and not from the manual records. Businesses must make sure that any data transferred is done accurately.

Incorrect set up of the accounting software

It is important that the software is set up appropriately for any special scheme such as the flat rate scheme, cash accounting scheme or annual scheme. Failure to do this would lead to an incorrect VAT return.

Note that if there are errors in data entered into the accounting system this will lead to errors in the VAT return, for example if the wrong rate of VAT is input into the system then this will flow through and create an incorrect VAT return.

2.3 Pro-forma VAT control account

Given below is a pro-forma VAT control account. Numbers have been omitted for clarity.

1 January 2024 to 31 March 2024			
VAT deductible – input tax	£ p	**VAT payable – output tax**	£ p
VAT you have been charged on your purchases		VAT you have charged on your sales	
January	X	January	X
February	X	February	X
March	X	March	X
Postponed accounting import VAT	X	Postponed accounting import VAT	X
Adjustments of previous errors (if within the error limit – Chapter 7)			
Net overclaim of input tax from previous returns	X	Net understatement of output tax on previous returns	X
Bad debt relief (section 2.6)	X		
Subtotal	X	Subtotal	X
Less: VAT on credits received from suppliers (e.g. credit notes received)	(X)	Less: VAT on credits allowed to customers (e.g. credit notes issued)	(X)
Total tax deductible	X	Total tax payable	X
		Less: Total tax deductible	(X)
		Payable to HMRC	X
Bank	X		

The VAT control account is part of the business's double entry bookkeeping system.

However, the VAT on credit notes received in this example is deducted from input tax and the VAT on credit notes issued is deducted from output tax instead of being credited and debited respectively.

This is because this is how credit notes are dealt with in the VAT return.

However, businesses do not have to prepare a VAT control account in exactly this way.

Test your understanding 1

Aditi runs a small business making only standard-rated supplies. The balance due to HMRC per her VAT control account is £3,472.56.

She subsequently discovers the following errors:

1   She has recorded a credit note due to a customer of £81 including VAT, as a credit note from a supplier.

2   A purchase invoice of £420 including VAT has been omitted from the purchase daybook.

After these corrections have been made, what is the corrected balance of VAT due to HMRC?

A   £3,389.06

B   £3,375.56

C   £3,429.56

D   £3,569.56

 Test your understanding 2

Lendl runs a small business making only standard-rated supplies.

The balance of VAT repayable by HMRC in Lendl's VAT control account is £2,246.39. However, when he completes his draft VAT return it shows VAT repayable of only £1,976.75.

Lendl checks his figures and finds one error.

Which of the following is the error that explains the difference?

A   VAT recoverable on purchases is recorded as £5,140.62 in the VAT control account but has been entered as £5,410.26 in the draft VAT return calculations.

B   Lendl issued a credit note to a customer of £808.92 including VAT. The VAT has been correctly dealt with in the VAT control account but in the draft VAT return workings it has been treated as a credit note from a supplier.

2.4 Information required for the VAT return

Boxes 1 to 4 of the draft VAT return can be completed from the information in the VAT account. However, Boxes 6 and 7 require figures for total sales and purchases excluding VAT.

This information will need to be extracted from the original verified (preferably audited) ledger account totals posted up from the accounting records such as the sales daybook and purchases day book totals. It is also possible that information relating to VAT could be shown in a journal.

Therefore, the accounting records should be designed in such a way that these figures can also be easily identified.

You are not required to complete a VAT return in your assessment, however you are required to review a draft return from accounting information provided and verify the VAT return.

 Test your understanding 3

You are preparing the draft VAT return for Panther Alarms Ltd.

You must first complete the double entry for a few items to enable you to complete the VAT account and then extract the information you need to complete the draft VAT return.

Here is a list of possible sources of accounting information.

1   Sales daybook

2   Sales returns daybook

3   Bad and doubtful debts account (or impairment losses account)

4   Purchase returns daybook

5   Drawings account

6   Purchases daybook

7   Cash book

8   Assets account

9   Petty cash book

Enter the appropriate number from the list above against each item in the following list to show the best sources of information for the figures required.

If you think the information will be in more than one place then give the number for both.

Figures required to complete the draft VAT return:

A   sales

B   cash sales

C   credit notes issued

D   purchases

E   cash purchases

F   credit notes received

G   capital goods sold

H   capital goods purchased

I   bad debt relief

 Example

Thompson Brothers Ltd has voluntarily registered for VAT. Given below is its VAT account for the second VAT quarter of 2024.

Thompson Brothers Ltd
1 April 2024 to 30 June 2024

VAT deductible – input tax		**VAT payable – output tax**	
VAT on purchases	£	VAT on sales	£
April	700.00	April	1,350.00
May	350.00	May	1,750.00
June	350.00	June	700.00
	————		————
	1,400.00		3,800.00
Other adjustments			
Less: Credit notes received	(20.00)	Less: Credit notes issued	(120.00)
	————		————
Total tax deductible	1,380.00	Total tax payable	3,680.00
		Less: Total tax deductible	(1,380.00)
			————
		Payable to HMRC	2,300.00
			————

You are also given the summarised totals from the daybooks for the three-month period:

Sales daybook

	Net £	VAT £	Total £
Standard-rated	19,000.00	3,800.00	22,800.00
Zero-rated	800.00	–	800.00

Sales returns daybook

	Net £	VAT £	Total £
Standard-rated	600.00	120.00	720.00
Zero-rated	40.00	–	40.00

Purchases daybook

	Net £	VAT £	Total £
Standard-rated	7,000.00	1,400.00	8,400.00
Zero-rated	2,000.00	–	2,000.00

Purchases returns daybook

	Net £	VAT £	Total £
Standard-rated	100.00	20.00	120.00
Zero-rated	–	–	–

We are now in a position to complete the draft VAT return.

Solution

Step 1

Fill in Box 1 with the VAT on sales, less the VAT on credit notes issued.

This can be taken either from the VAT account or from the daybook summaries:
(£3,800.00 – £120.00) = £3,680.00.

Note that the figures in Boxes 1 – 5 you should include pence so put '.00' at the end if there are no pence in the total.

Step 2

Box 2 is for transactions in Northern Ireland with EU member states. This is outside the scope of the syllabus. It will always be zero in your assessment.

Note that for Boxes 1 – 5, if there is no entry for a box, '0.00' should be put in the box.

Step 3

Complete Box 3 with the total of Boxes 1 and 2:
(£3,680.00 + £0.00) = £3,680.00.

Step 4

Fill in Box 4 with the total of VAT on all purchases, less the total VAT on any credit notes received.

These figures can be taken either from the VAT account, or from the daybook totals:
(£1,400.00 – £20.00) = £1,380.00.

Step 5

Complete Box 5 by deducting the figure in Box 4 from the total in Box 3:
(£3,680.00 – £1,380.00) = £2,300.00.

This is the amount due to HMRC and should equal the balance on the VAT account.

If the Box 4 figure is larger than the Box 3 total then there is more input tax reclaimable than output tax to pay – this means that this is the amount being reclaimed from HMRC.

Step 6

Fill in Box 6 with the VAT-exclusive figure of all sales less credit notes issued.

In this example the information will come from the day books:
(£19,000 + £800 – £600 – £40) = £19,160

Note that this figure includes zero-rated supplies and any exempt supplies that are made.

Note that the figures in Boxes 6 – 9 should be whole pounds only. In the assessment, it does not matter if the numbers are rounded up or down.

Step 7

Fill in Box 7 with the VAT-exclusive total of all purchases less credit notes received.

Again, in this example this will be taken from the day books:
(£7,000 + £2,000 – £100) = £8,900

Step 8

Boxes 8 and 9 are for transactions in Northern Ireland with EU member states. These are outside the scope of the syllabus.

Note that for Boxes 6 – 9, if there is no entry for any box then '0' should be put in the box. Leaving these boxes blank in the assessment will lose you marks.

Step 9

If VAT is due to HMRC then payment must be made in accordance with the usual time limits. For assessment purposes, you may be asked to state the payment date, or complete an email advising when this amount will be paid.

		£
VAT due on sales and other outputs	**Box 1**	3,680.00
VAT due on acquisitions of goods made in Northern Ireland from EU Member States	**Box 2**	0.00
Total VAT due (the sum of boxes 1 and 2)	**Box 3**	3,680.00
VAT reclaimed on purchases and other inputs, (including acquisitions in Northern Ireland from EU member states)	**Box 4**	1,380.00
Net VAT to be paid to Customs by you (Difference between boxes 3 and 4)	**Box 5**	2,300.00
Total value of sales and all other outputs excluding any VAT.	**Box 6**	19,160
Total value of purchases and all other inputs excluding any VAT.	**Box 7**	8,900
Total value of dispatches of goods and related costs, excluding VAT, from Northern Ireland to EU Member States	**Box 8**	0
Total value of acquisitions of goods and related costs, excluding VAT, made in Northern Ireland from EU Member States	**Box 9**	0

If the business makes sales or purchases for cash, then the relevant net and VAT figures from the cash receipts and payments books and petty cash book should also be included on the VAT return.

Test your understanding 4

Given below is the summary of relevant ledger accounts for a business for the three months ended 31 March 2024. The business has voluntarily registered for VAT.

Sales and sales returns account					
Date 2024	**Reference**	**Debit £**	**Date 2024**	**Reference**	**Credit £**
1/1 to 31/03	SRDB Std-rated	1,625.77	1/1 to 31/03	SDB Std-rated	15,485.60
1/1 to 31/03	SRDB Zero-rated	106.59	1/1 to 31/03	SDB Zero-rated	1,497.56
31/03	Bal c/d	15,250.80			
	Total	16,983.16		Total	16,983.16

Purchases and purchase returns account					
Date 2024	**Reference**	**Debit £**	**Date 2024**	**Reference**	**Credit £**
1/1 to 31/03	PDB Std-rated	8,127.45	1/1 to 31/03	PRDB Std-rated	935.47
1/1 to 31/03	PDB Zero-rated	980.57	1/1 to 31/03	PRDB Zero-rated	80.40
			31/03	Bal c/d	8,092.15
	Total	9,108.02		Total	9,108.02

VAT account					
Date 2024	**Reference**	**Debit £**	**Date 2024**	**Reference**	**Credit £**
31/03	PDB	1,625.49	31/03	SDB	3,097.12
31/03	SRDB	325.15	31/03	PRDB	187.09
	Bal c/d	1,333.57			
	Total	3,284.21		Total	3,284.21

Abbreviations key

SDB – sales daybook, SDRB – sales returns day book

PDB – purchases daybook, PRDB – purchase returns day book

Required

Prepare the VAT return for the quarter ended 31 March 2024.

		£
VAT due sales and other outputs	**Box 1**	
VAT due on acquisitions of goods made in Northern Ireland from EU Member States	**Box 2**	
Total VAT due (the sum of boxes 1 and 2)	**Box 3**	
VAT reclaimed on purchases and other inputs, (including acquisitions in Northern Ireland from EU Member States)	**Box 4**	
Net VAT to be paid to HMRC (Difference between boxes 3 and 4)	**Box 5**	
Total value of sales and all other outputs excluding any VAT.	**Box 6**	
Total value of purchases and all other inputs excluding any VAT.	**Box 7**	

2.5   Purchase of items with non-recoverable VAT

When a business spends money on UK customer entertaining and cars with some private use, they cannot recover any input VAT (Chapter 4). VAT on these items must not be included in the input VAT recoverable in Box 4 of the draft return.

If a business buys zero-rated items there will not be any VAT to include in Box 4.

There are different views on how the purchases of these items should be dealt with in Box 7 of the return. However, for this assessment the VAT-exclusive figure for all purchases, including zero-rated purchases and items on which VAT cannot be recovered, **is included** in Box 7.

2.6   VAT: Bad debt relief

You will notice that there is an entry in the pro-forma VAT control account for bad debt relief as additional input tax.

When a supplier invoices a customer for an amount including VAT, the supplier must pay the VAT to HMRC. If the customer then fails to pay the debt, the supplier's position is that output VAT has been paid, but never collected. This is seemingly unfair, so an adjustment is allowed, for the supplier to recover such amounts.

Suppliers **cannot issue credit notes** to recover VAT on irrecoverable debts (bad debts). Instead, the business must make an **adjustment through the VAT return**. The business can reclaim VAT already paid if:

- output tax was paid on the original supply

- six months have elapsed between the date payment was due (or the date of supply if later) and the date of the VAT return, and

- the debt has been written off as a bad debt in the accounting records

- the debt is between six months and four years and six months old

- the debt has not been sold to a factoring company

- the business did not charge more than the selling price for the items.

If the business receives a **repayment of the debt later**, it must adjust the VAT relief claimed.

The bad debt relief is an expense of the business and so the VAT in respect of the sale is treated as recoverable input VAT. It is included in Box 4 of the draft return along with the VAT on purchases.

When computing the VAT on the bad debt check carefully to identify if the amount of the bad debt given in the question is VAT-inclusive. This is likely because the amount the customer owes is the amount that includes VAT.

To calculate the VAT for a VAT-inclusive debt, you should multiply the bad debt by 20/120 (or 1/6) for standard-rated items. If the question uses the term 'bad debt relief is to be claimed' it is the VAT to be claimed which is given to you.

On the cessation of a business, a claim can be made for relief on all outstanding debts up to the date of cessation.

If a business is bought by another business as a going concern, and the VAT registration of the target business is transferred to the acquiring business, it is possible to claim bad debt relief for bad debts of the target business.

Example

A business has made purchases of £23,700 (net of VAT) in the VAT quarter and has written off a bad debt of £750 (including VAT).

It also has a net under claim of VAT of £1,250.00 from earlier periods.

Calculate the figure that will be entered on the draft VAT return for the quarter in Box 4.

Solution

	£	£ p
Purchases (net of VAT)	23,700	
VAT (£23,700 × 20%)		4,740.00
Bad debt	750	
VAT (£750 × 20/120)		125.00
Net under claim of VAT		1,250.00
		_____
Total VAT for Box 4		6,115.00
		_____

 Test your understanding 5

Jonas wrote off a bad debt on 3 June 2024.

The goods had been delivered to the customer on 14 February 2024 and the invoice was due for payment on 15 March 2024.

Jonas does not use the cash accounting scheme.

What is the earliest that VAT can be claimed?

A   Quarter ending 31 May 2024

B   Quarter ending 31 August 2024

C   Quarter ending 30 November 2024

D   Quarter ending 28 February 2025

Test your understanding 6

You are provided with the following summary of Mark Ambrose's books and other information provided by Mark for the quarter ended 30 September 2024. Mark is a seasonal trader who has voluntarily registered for VAT.

MARK AMBROSE

Summary of day books and petty cash expenditure
Quarter ended 30 September 2024

Sales daybook

	Work done £	VAT £	Total £
July	12,900.00	2,580.00	15,480.00
August	13,200.00	2,640.00	15,840.00
September	12,300.00	2,460.00	14,760.00
	38,400.00	7,680.00	46,080.00

Purchase daybook

	Net £	VAT £	Total £
July	5,250.00	1,050.00	6,300.00
August	5,470.00	1,094.00	6,564.00
September	5,750.00	1,150.00	6,900.00
	16,470.00	3,294.00	19,764.00

On 30 September 2024, Mark purchased a car for £8,400 including VAT.

This car is to be used by Mark for business and private purposes.

The purchase of the car has not yet been recorded in the books.

Bad debts list – 30 September 2024

Date debt due	Customer	Total (including VAT)
30 November 2023	High Melton Farms	£300.00
3 January 2024	Concorde Motors	£180.00
4 April 2024	Bawtry Engineering	£120.00

These have now been written off as bad debts.

Complete boxes 1 to 9 of the draft VAT return for the quarter ended 30 September 2024.

		£
VAT due sales and other outputs	**Box 1**	
VAT due on acquisitions of goods made in Northern Ireland from EU Member States	**Box 2**	
Total VAT due (the sum of boxes 1 and 2)	**Box 3**	
VAT reclaimed on purchases and other inputs, (including acquisitions in Northern Ireland from EU Member States)	**Box 4**	
Net VAT to be paid to HMRC (Difference between boxes 3 and 4)	**Box 5**	
Total value of sales and all other outputs excluding any VAT.	**Box 6**	
Total value of purchases and all other inputs excluding any VAT.	**Box 7**	
Total value of dispatches of goods and related costs, excluding any VAT, from Northern Ireland to EU Member States	**Box 8**	
Total value of acquisitions of goods and related costs, excluding any VAT, made in Northern Ireland from EU Member States	**Box 9**	

Reference material

Information on bad debt relief can be found in the 'Bad debt and VAT' section of your reference material provided in the real assessment, so you do not need to learn it.

Why not look up the correct part of the reference material in the introduction to this text book now?

3 Overseas aspects of VAT

3.1 Exports of goods

Goods sold by a UK VAT registered business to a customer in another country are known as exports. Since the place of supply is the country where the goods came from, the UK supplier must charge UK VAT. The customer's own state may tax the goods as well, but this is not covered in your assessment.

Exports of taxable goods are always zero-rated, even if they would have had a different rate of VAT if they had been delivered to a UK customer. Therefore, they are accounted for on the VAT return in the same way as any other zero-rated sale. As no VAT needs to be charged, there will be no output tax to include in VAT return Box 1. However, the value of the export sale is included in the taxable supplies total in VAT return Box 6.

Because exports of are all zero-rated taxable supplies, this means (applying the usual input VAT recovery principles – Chapter 4) that the UK business can reclaim all UK input VAT that it suffers on its own expenses or purchases attributable to the export business.

Being a regular exporter of goods, particularly if the related 'cost of sales' items are standard-rated when purchased, is a common reason for a UK business to be a net reclaimer of VAT in its normal trading.

To prevent false claims about non-existent exports, it is a condition for zero-rating of any export supply, that documentary evidence of export is obtained and retained by the UK taxable business which did zero-rate.

Evidence of export means the UK supplier must keep evidence of delivery of the identified goods to a non-UK address. This may be a different address from the final customer's address (such as an intermediate handling agent), as long as it is evidence of delivery made outside the UK.

Example

Bettrys runs a UK business selling standard-rated pet accessories. The business has voluntarily registered for VAT.

Bettrys sells some items overseas. In the quarter ended 31 December 2024, her sales are as follows:

	£
Sales to UK customers	2,740
Sales to overseas customers	1,370

All these figures exclude VAT.

What are the figures that are included in Boxes 1 and 6 of the draft VAT return?

Solution

		£
Box 1	VAT on standard-rated sales 20% × (£2,740)	548.00
Box 6	Value of all sales including exports (£2,740 + £1,370)	4,110

3.2 Imports of goods

Goods bought by a UK VAT registered business from a supplier in another country are known as imports. When the goods cross the UK border and enter the UK via the legal UK Customs point at any UK airport, seaport, or when passing through the Channel Tunnel, UK import VAT is levied as a form of customs duty. This means that the importer is liable to pay a duty equal to the same amount of VAT that would have been payable if the same goods were purchased from a supplier in the UK. The aim is to treat foreign goods for VAT in the same way as home-produced goods, and to collect the same VAT on them, once they enter the country.

The import VAT amount will be reclaimed in Box 4, as recoverable input VAT and the value of goods on which import VAT was paid will be included in Box 7.

Example

Warhorse Ltd is a UK business selling standard-rated horse-riding accessories. The company started trading on 1 April 2024 and voluntarily registered for VAT.

The company imports some items from overseas.

In its first quarter ended 30 June 2024, the details of purchases are as follows:

	£
Purchases from UK businesses	3,125
Purchases from overseas businesses	2,350

All these figures exclude VAT.

What are the figures to include in the draft VAT return for Boxes 4 and 7?

Solution

		£
Box 4	VAT on purchases plus VAT on imports 20% × (£3,125 + £2,350)	1,095.00
Box 7	All purchases including imports (£3,125 + £2,350)	5,475

3.3 Postponed accounting

UK VAT registered businesses do not have to pay their own import VAT duties at the border, but may opt to delay accounting for UK import VAT on business imports of goods until the next usual VAT return.

This is known as postponed accounting.

On its next VAT return, the UK business will account for the liability to pay the import VAT within the VAT control account. It is therefore included in the VAT return **Box 1**, which increases the amount of output VAT.

However, the same import VAT can normally be reclaimed in full on the same VAT return (as long as the business is not making any supplies on which input VAT is not recoverable). The import VAT figure is also included in the VAT control account as recoverable VAT. It is therefore also included in the total recoverable input VAT in return **Box 4**.

There is no overall impact on the VAT liability shown in **Box 5** in most cases.

The value of the imports on which import VAT is reclaimed is also included in the **Box 7** figure for total purchases and other inputs.

However, the total value of imports on which output VAT was accounted for in Box 1, is **not included in Box 6**. The reason is that Box 6 is for totalling supplies – both taxable supplies and deemed supplies (for example fuel scale charges). Under the place of supply rules an import of goods is not treated as UK supply, it is an import event separately charged to UK VAT.

 Example

Morag voluntarily registered for VAT. She imports goods which would be standard-rated if bought in the UK and has opted to use postponed accounting for VAT on imports.

All the goods she sells are standard-rated items.

In the quarter ended 31 December 2024 she makes sales and purchases as follows:

	£
Sales to UK businesses	6,000
Export sales	2,240
Purchases from UK businesses	4,850
Imports	2,000

All these figures exclude VAT.

What are the figures to include in Boxes 1, 4, 6 and 7 of her draft VAT return?

Solution

		£
Box 1	VAT on standard-rated sales plus VAT on imports	
	20% × (£6,000 + £2,000)	1,600.00
Box 4	VAT on purchases plus VAT on imports	
	20% × (£4,850 + £2,000)	1,370.00
Box 6	Value of all sales including exports	
	(£6,000 + £2,240)	8,240
Box 7	All purchases including imports	
	(£4,850 + £2,000)	6,850

The export sales are zero-rated so there is no VAT on them to include in Box 1. However, both UK and export sales values are included in Box 6.

Imports are treated like normal UK purchases in the goods value entered in Box 7, and for the recoverable input VAT value entered in Box 4.

Test your understanding 7

Tomlin Ltd has voluntarily registered for VAT.

The following accounts have been extracted from its ledgers.

Date		Dr	Cr
		£	£
Sales: UK			
30.6.24	Sales daybook		4,050
31.7.24	Sales daybook		8,950
31.8 24	Sales daybook		2,210
Sales: Export			
30.6.24	Sales daybook		1,515
31.7.24	Sales daybook		2,058
31.8 24	Sales daybook		1,789
Purchases: UK			
30.6.24	Purchases daybook	3,460	
31.7.24	Purchases daybook	3,160	
31.8 24	Purchases daybook	3,370	
VAT: Output tax			
30.6.24	Sales daybook		810.00
31.7.24	Sales daybook		1,790.00
31.8 24	Sales daybook		442.00
VAT: Input tax			
30.6.24	Purchases daybook	692.00	
31.7.24	Purchases daybook	632.00	
31.8 24	Purchases daybook	674.00	

Bad debt relief on a sales invoice for £600 including VAT is to be claimed this quarter.

Verify whether the entries have been correctly made in the following draft VAT form 100 for the period. If you find any errors, list the errors and then correct the entries.

		£
VAT due sales and other outputs	**Box 1**	3,642.00
VAT due on acquisitions of goods made in Northern Ireland from EU Member States	**Box 2**	0.00
Total VAT due (the sum of boxes 1 and 2)	**Box 3**	3,642.00
VAT reclaimed on purchases and other inputs, (including acquisitions in Northern Ireland from the EU Member States)	**Box 4**	2,598.00
Net VAT to be paid to HMRC (Difference between boxes 3 and 4)	**Box 5**	1,044.00
Total value of sales and all other outputs excluding any VAT.	**Box 6**	19,057
Total value of purchases and all other inputs excluding any VAT.	**Box 7**	9,990
Total value of dispatches of goods and related costs, excluding any VAT, from Northern Ireland to EU Member States	**Box 8**	0
Total value of acquisitions of goods and related costs, excluding any VAT, made in Northern Ireland from EU Member States	**Box 9**	0

Test your understanding 8

Manaccan Ltd is a UK resident company and is VAT registered. It has been importing computers from China since 1 January 2025 and uses postponed accounting for imports.

Manaccan Ltd makes only taxable supplies. For the quarter ended 31 March 2025 imports of £100,000 have been made. This amount excludes any VAT.

Explain how Manaccan Ltd will have to account for VAT on the computers imported from China.

3.4 Place of supply

The place of supply rules are needed to decide whether a supply of goods or services involving a UK business and either a supplier or customer outside the UK, is treated as a supply occurring under the UK VAT system.

For a supply of:

Goods The place of supply is the country **where the goods come from**.

For a supply of:

Services (a) **Business to business** (B2B)

(i.e. supplies to customers who are themselves in business)

The place of supply is where the **customer is based**.

So, if a UK business receives any supply of services from a non-UK supplier, the services are deemed to be supplied in the UK under the UK VAT system, and liable to UK VAT.

If a UK business supplies services to a non-UK business customer, the services are deemed to be supplied outside the UK and are therefore outside the UK VAT system, and not liable to UK VAT.

(b) **Business to consumer** (B2C)

(i.e. supplies to customers who give no evidence to the supplier of being in business)

The place of supply is where the **supplier is based**.

Therefore, if a UK business supplies services to an overseas customer and can find no evidence that that customer is in business, the place of supply is the UK, and UK VAT must be applied by the seller, and shown on a UK tax invoice. In fact, the UK supplier treats this B2C services sale for VAT just as it would treat a UK buyer of the services.

There are exceptions to the above general rules for certain services, such as digital downloads, and land-related services, but these are not covered by your assessment.

3.5 Supplies of services by a UK supplier

Under the place of supply rules, **business to business (B2B) supplies of services** are treated as a supply made in the country where the **customer is based**. This means that from the UK supplier's perspective the supply is treated as outside the scope of UK VAT. The supplier will not have to account for any UK output VAT, but will still include the amount charged in Box 6 of the VAT return.

Supplies of services to a **non-business customer (B2C)** (e.g. an individual) are treated as a supply made in the country where the **supplier is based**. This means that from the UK supplier's perspective VAT is applied in the normal way just as if the supply is made within the UK. In the VAT return these supplies are treated like any other sale, i.e. include output VAT in Box 1 and sales in Box 6. There are exceptions to this rule but they are not covered by your assessment.

3.6 Services supplied to UK businesses from overseas – the reverse charge

Under the place of supply rules, **B2B supplies of services** are treated as a supply made in the country where the **customer is based**. This means that if a UK business is supplied with services by an overseas supplier, the UK business customer must account for UK VAT on the services. This is known as the '**reverse charge**' procedure.

On its VAT return, the purchasing business treats the purchase as if it had supplied the services to itself, and accounts for output VAT at the right UK rate (which is nearly always the 20% standard rate).

The UK business therefore includes the output VAT on the reverse charged supply, with other VAT on sales, in **Box 1** of the VAT return. The same VAT is also included (assuming it is all recoverable) as input VAT on UK purchases, in **Box 4** of the return.

The value of the supply itself (excluding the VAT) must then be included in both **Box 6** (value of sales) and **Box 7** (value of purchases).

 Example

Geraint runs a UK VAT-registered business. He buys services from overseas, which would be standard-rated if bought in the UK. In the quarter ended 31 December 2024 he buys services totalling £2,600 excluding VAT.

What are the figures to include in Boxes 1, 4, 6 and 7 in respect of these services in the draft VAT return?

Solution

		£
Box 1	VAT on standard-rated sales	
	20% × £2,600	520.00
Box 4	VAT on purchases	520.00
Box 6	Sales	2,600
Box 7	Purchases	2,600

 Test your understanding 9

You are required to complete a draft VAT return for Coleman Ltd in respect of the quarter ended 31 December 2024. Coleman Ltd has voluntarily registered for VAT.

You are given the following information to assist you in this task:

1 Sales of £9,160 were made during the quarter ended 31 December 2024, of which a total of £650 relates to exports and the remainder was standard-rated sales to UK customers. All sales figures given exclude VAT.

2 Total purchases by the company in the quarter amounted to £3,100 of standard-rated inputs from UK suppliers, and £230 of imported goods. Coleman Ltd uses postponed accounting in relation to imports.

3 The sales figures for October 2024 include an invoice for standard-rated goods with a value, excluding VAT, of £320.

   These goods were actually despatched in September 2024 and should have been accounted for in the VAT return for the previous quarter, but were omitted in error.

4 A debt of £66, inclusive of VAT, was written off as bad during the month of December 2024.

   The related sale was made in February 2024. Bad debt relief is now to be claimed.

Prepare the following draft VAT form 100 for the period.

		£
VAT due sales and other outputs	**Box 1**	
VAT due on acquisitions of goods made in Northern Ireland from EU Member States	**Box 2**	
Total VAT due (the sum of boxes 1 and 2)	**Box 3**	
VAT reclaimed on purchases and other inputs, including to Northern Ireland from EU Member States	**Box 4**	
Net VAT to be paid to HMRC by you (Difference between boxes 3 and 4)	**Box 5**	
Total value of sales and all other outputs excluding any VAT.	**Box 6**	
Total value of purchases and all other inputs excluding any VAT.	**Box 7**	
Total value of dispatches of goods and related costs, excluding any VAT, from Northern Ireland to EU Member States	**Box 8**	
Total value of acquisitions of goods and related costs, excluding any VAT, made in Northern Ireland from EU Member States	**Box 9**	

Reference material

Information about overseas VAT can be found in the 'International trade and VAT' section of your reference material provided in the real assessment, so you do not need to learn it.

Why not look up the correct part of the reference material in the introduction to this text book now?

4 Summary

In this chapter, the completion of the draft VAT return was considered. A business using digital accounting software will have a VAT control account which summarises all of the VAT from the accounting records. Information is transferred from the VAT control account to complete the first five boxes on the draft VAT return. So the figure for VAT due to or from HMRC on the draft VAT return should equal the balance on the VAT account.

In order to complete the remaining boxes on the draft VAT return information will be required from the daybooks within the accounting records of the business.

The rules for a UK VAT registered business's sales to overseas customers and purchases can be summarised as follows for a UK business that only makes standard-rated sales and purchases (when the supply is wholly in the UK).

Goods

Type of transaction	Treatment on VAT return	
Sales to outside the UK (exports)	Zero-rated	No VAT to show in Box 1 Include the sales value in Box 6
Purchases from outside the UK (imports)	Standard-rated (for import duty type of VAT),)	Include the VAT suffered in Box 4 Include the purchases (imports) net-of-VAT value in Box 7
	Assume that postponed accounting for Import VAT is used by the UK importer	Include the import VAT in Box 1 BUT Do not include the value of imports in Box 6, as they are not taxable supplies, as postponed import VAT is not a reverse charge on supply

Services

Type of transaction	Treatment on VAT return	
B2B sales to overseas customers	Outside scope of VAT	Include sales value in Box 6
B2C sales to overseas customers	Standard-rated	Include as a sale and put output VAT in Box 1 and the net sales value in Box 6
B2B purchases from overseas suppliers	Reverse charge (treat as a sale that the business makes to itself)	Calculate VAT at the UK rate and show this in box 1 Include the same amount of VAT in Box 4 Include purchase value in Box 6 as a reverse charge supply, and separately show this figure in Box 7 as a purchase

Test your understanding answers

 ### Test your understanding 1

The correct answer is B.

The credit note due to a customer includes VAT of £13.50 (£81 × 20/120). If posted correctly this reduces output VAT. This has been included on the wrong side of the VAT account and hence is increasing the output VAT. It must be posted twice to the other side of the account to correct it. This has the effect of reducing the VAT due to HMRC by £27.

The purchase invoice includes VAT of £70 (£420 × 20/120). Including this in the VAT account will increase input VAT and hence reduce the VAT due to HMRC.

The net reduction is £97 (£27 + £70).

The corrected balance is therefore £3,375.56 (£3,472.56 – £97)

 ### Test your understanding 2

The correct answer is B.

The VAT return is showing £269.64 (£2,246.39 – £1,976.75) less VAT repayable than it should. It is important to note that this figure is the amount REPAYABLE not PAYABLE. Therefore, we are looking for an error that has overstated output tax or understated input tax.

Error A would mean that input VAT was overstated on the VAT return by £269.64 (£5,410.26 – £5,140.62), increasing the VAT repayable.

Error B – if treated correctly, a credit note to a customer reduces output tax. Lendl's error means that input tax has been decreased in the VAT return workings instead. This would make VAT repayable lower than it should be. In order to correct this, output tax must be decreased by twice the error i.e. £269.64 (£808.92 × 20/120 × 2).

Test your understanding 3

A	Sales	1
B	Cash sales	7
C	Credit notes issued	2
D	Purchases	6
E	Cash purchases	7 and 9
F	Credit notes received	4
G	Capital goods sold	8 or 1 (if an analysed sales day book)
H	Capital goods purchased	8 or 6 (if analysed)
I	Bad debt relief	3

Test your understanding 4

		£
VAT due sales and other outputs	Box 1	2,771.97
VAT due on acquisitions of goods made in Northern Ireland from EU Member States	Box 2	0.00
Total VAT due (the sum of boxes 1 and 2)	Box 3	2,771.97
VAT reclaimed on purchases and other inputs, (including acquisitions in Northern Ireland from EU member states)	Box 4	1,438.40
Net VAT to be paid to HMRC (Difference between boxes 3 and 4)	Box 5	1,333.57
Total value of sales and all other outputs excluding any VAT.	Box 6	15,250
Total value of purchases and all other inputs excluding any VAT.	Box 7	8,092
Total value of dispatches of goods and related costs, excluding any VAT, from Northern Ireland to EU Member States	Box 8	0
Total value of acquisitions of goods and related costs, excluding any VAT, made in Northern Ireland from EU Member States	Box 9	0

Workings

Box 1	£
VAT on sales	3,097.12
Less: VAT on credit notes	(325.15)
	2,771.97

Box 4	£
VAT on purchases	1,625.49
Less: VAT on credit notes	(187.09)
	1,438.40

Box 6	£
Standard-rated sales	15,485.60
Zero-rated sales	1,497.56
	16,983.16
Less: Credit notes	
Standard-rated	(1,625.77)
Zero-rated	(106.59)
Balance on sales & sales returns account	15,250.80

Round down to £15,250

Box 7	£
Standard-rated purchases	8,127.45
Zero-rated purchases	980.57
	9,108.02
Less: Credit notes	
Standard-rated	(935.47)
Zero-rated	(80.40)
Balance on purchase & purchase returns account	8,092.15

Test your understanding 5

The correct answer is C.

Bad debt relief can be claimed after 6 months has elapsed from the date payment was due (or the date of supply if later).

In this case, 6 months after 15 March 2024 is 15 September 2024, which falls into the quarter ended 30 November 2024.

Test your understanding 6

		£
VAT due sales and other outputs	Box 1	7,680.00
VAT due on acquisitions of goods made in Northern Ireland from EU Member States	Box 2	0.00
Total VAT due (the sum of boxes 1 and 2)	Box 3	7,680.00
VAT reclaimed on purchases and other inputs, (including acquisitions in Northern Ireland from EU Member States)	Box 4	3,374.00
Net VAT to be paid to HMRC (Difference between boxes 3 and 4)	Box 5	4,306.00
Total value of sales and all other outputs excluding any VAT.	Box 6	38,400
Total value of purchases and all other inputs excluding any VAT.	Box 7	23,470
Total value of dispatches of goods and related costs, excluding any VAT, from Northern Ireland to EU Member States	Box 8	0
Total value of acquisitions of goods and related costs, excluding any VAT, made in Northern Ireland from EU Member States	Box 9	0

Workings for VAT return

		£
Box 4:	From PDB	3,294.00
	Bad debts (Note)	80.00
		3,374.00

		£
Box 7:	From PDB	16,470
	New car (£8,400 × 100/120)	7,000
		23,470

Note: Bad debts more than six months old = (£300.00 + £180.00) = £480.00

VAT = (20/120 × £480.00) = £80.00

☼ Test your understanding 7

		£
VAT due **on sales** and other outputs – £3,642 was an **ERROR** – should be £810 + £1,790 + £442 = £3,042	**Box 1**	3,042.00
VAT due in the period on acquisitions of goods made in Northern Ireland from EU Member States – **CORRECT**	**Box 2**	0.00
Total VAT due (the sum of boxes 1 and 2) – £3,642 was an **ERROR,** due to the Box 1 error.	**Box 3**	3,042.00
VAT reclaimed on purchases and other inputs (including to Northern Ireland from EU Member States) – £2,598 was an **ERROR** – the bad debt adjustment is only £100 so the corrected input VAT total = £692 + £632 + £674 + £100 = £2,098.	**Box 4**	2,098.00
Net VAT to be paid to HMRC (Difference between boxes 3 and 4) **now corrected** in line with changes to Boxes 3 and 4.	**Box 5**	944.00
Total value of sales and all other outputs excluding any VAT. £19,057 was an **ERROR** as the June exports were omitted. Should be £4,050 + £8,950 + £2,210 + £1,515 + £2,058 + £1,789 = £20,572.	**Box 6**	20,572
Total value of purchases and all other inputs excluding any VAT. This figure was **CORRECT** (£3,460 + £3,160 + £3,370).	**Box 7**	9,990
Total value of intra-community dispatches of goods and related costs, excluding any VAT, from Northern Ireland to EU Member States – **CORRECT**	**Box 8**	0
Total value of intra-community acquisitions of goods and related costs, excluding any VAT, made in Northern Ireland from EU Member States – **CORRECT**	**Box 9**	0

Test your understanding 8

On the quarter ended 31 March 2025 VAT return, Manaccan Ltd will add total import VAT of £100,000 × 20% = £20,000 to Box 1, which increases the amount of output VAT.

However, the same import VAT is reclaimed in full on the same VAT return by adding £20,000 of import VAT to total recoverable input VAT entered in Box 4.

The value of the imports on which import VAT is reclaimed (£100,000) is also included in the Box 7 figure for total purchases and other inputs.

 Test your understanding 9

		£
VAT due on sales and other outputs	**Box 1**	1,748.00
VAT due on acquisitions of goods made in Northern Ireland from EU Member States	**Box 2**	0.00
Total VAT due (the sum of boxes 1 and 2)	**Box 3**	1,748.00
VAT reclaimed on purchases and other inputs, (including acquisitions to Northern Ireland from EU Member States)	**Box 4**	677.00
Net VAT to be paid to HMRC (Difference between boxes 3 and 4)	**Box 5**	1,071.00
Total value of sales and all other outputs excluding any VAT.	**Box 6**	9,160
Total value of purchases and all other inputs excluding any VAT.	**Box 7**	3,330
Total value of dispatches of goods and related costs, excluding any VAT, from Northern Ireland to EU Member States	**Box 8**	0
Total value of acquisitions of goods and related costs, excluding any VAT, made in Northern Ireland from EU Member States	**Box 9**	0

Workings for VAT return

		£
Box 1:	Sales	9,160
	Imports under postponed accounting	230
	Less: Exports (zero-rated)	(650)
		————
	Standard-rated sales	8,740
		————
	Output VAT (£8,740 × 20%)	1,748.00
		————

		£
Box 4:	VAT on standard-rated purchases and imports ((£3,100 + £230) × 20%)	666.00
	Bad debt relief (£66 × 20/120)	11.00
		————
		677.00
		————

		£
Box 7:	Standard-rated inputs	3,100
	Zero-rated inputs	230
		————
		3,330
		————

Note that no adjustment is needed to the figures given in the question to calculate the numbers to be entered in the VAT return.

This is because the error does not need to be corrected by separate disclosure. The value of the error is below £10,000 so it can be corrected on this period's return.

Errors, penalties and communicating VAT information

7

Introduction

This chapter starts by covering errors. Mistakes and errors are easily made in any aspect of life, but when it comes to making errors on a VAT return there are certain steps to follow to address an error.

Penalties may be imposed for late filing and late payment, which we will learn about in this chapter.

There will be times, including when making an error, that businesses will have to communicate effectively to HMRC. In your assessment you may be asked to communicate information on VAT or payroll. In this chapter we will consider how to communicate VAT information effectively.

ASSESSMENT CRITERIA
Implications for non-compliance with VAT regulations (1.5)
VAT calculations (2.3)
Make adjustments for errors and omissions in VAT returns (3.1)
Verify information contained within VAT returns (3.2)
Communicating information on VAT related matters (5.1)

CONTENTS

1 Errors in returns
2 Late submission
3 Late payment
4 Further penalties
5 Communicating VAT information

1 Errors in returns

1.1 VAT: Adjustment of previous errors

If a trader makes an error in a VAT return which leads to net VAT payable being understated, this must be corrected.

A net VAT error is calculated as the difference between the additional VAT due to HMRC, less any VAT claimable by the trader.

You will notice in the pro-forma VAT control account (Chapter 6) that there are entries for net under claims and net over claims.

Net errors made in previous VAT returns that are below the disclosure threshold can be adjusted for on the VAT return through the VAT account.

The error disclosure threshold is later in section 1.3 of this chapter.

An error in the underlying records is corrected via a journal entry to the appropriate nominal ledger accounts which will include the VAT control account.

An error in the draft VAT return can be corrected by adjusting the relevant box on the draft return.

- A single error affecting **output tax** is adjusted by adding or subtracting it to **Box 1**.

- A single error affecting **input tax** is adjusted for in **Box 4**.

If there are several errors, they are netted off and the single figure for net errors will be entered on the draft return. This will be entered as additional input tax in Box 4 if there has been an earlier net under claim of VAT (if the business has paid too much VAT), or as additional output tax in Box 1 (if the business has paid too little VAT) if the net error was a net over claim in a previous return.

To summarise:

	Box 1	Box 4
Single error affecting output tax	✓	
Single error affecting input tax		✓
Net errors resulting in VAT over claimed in past	✓	
Net errors resulting in VAT under claimed in past		✓

1.2 Errors above the threshold

For deliberate errors or errors above the 'error correction threshold', the HMRC VAT Error Correction Team should be informed immediately either by a letter or on Form VAT 652. This is known as voluntary disclosure.

 Test your understanding 1

You are a self-employed accounting technician and Duncan Bye, a motor engineer, is one of your clients. He has voluntarily registered for VAT.

His records for the quarter ended 30 June 2024 showed the following:

Sales account					
Date 2024	Reference	Debit £	Date 2024	Reference	Credit £
			April	SDB	6,960.00
			May	SDB	6,510.00
			June	SDB	8,550.00
30/06	Bal c/d	22,020.00			
	Total	22,020.00		Total	22,020.00

Purchases account					
Date 2024	Reference	Debit £	Date 2024	Reference	Credit £
April	PDB	3,150.00			
May	PDB	3,270.00			
June	PDB	2,680.00			
			30/06	Bal c/d	9,100.00
	Total	9,100.00		Total	9,100.00

VAT account					
Date 2024	Reference	Debit £	Date 2024	Reference	Credit £
April	PDB	630.00	April	SDB	1,350.00
May	PDB	654.00	May	SDB	1,302.00
June	PDB	536.00	June	SDB	1,648.00
	Total			Total	

The VAT account has not yet been balanced off.

He also gives you some details of petty cash expenditure in the quarter, which has not yet been entered into the ledger.

	£ p
Net purchases	75.60
VAT	15.12
	90.72

Duncan understated his output VAT by £24 on his last return. This is to be corrected on his current return.

Prepare the following draft VAT return for the period.

		£
VAT due sales and other outputs	Box 1	
VAT due on acquisitions of goods made in Northern Ireland from EU Member States	Box 2	
Total VAT due (the sum of boxes 1 and 2)	Box 3	
VAT reclaimed on purchases and other inputs, (including acquisitions from the EU)	Box 4	
Net VAT to be paid to HMRC (Difference between boxes 3 and 4)	Box 5	
Total value of sales and all other outputs excluding any VAT.	Box 6	
Total value of purchases and all other inputs excluding any VAT.	Box 7	
Total value of dispatches of goods and related costs, excluding any VAT, from Northern Ireland to EU Member States	Box 8	
Total value of acquisitions of goods and related costs, excluding any VAT, made in Northern Ireland from EU Member States	Box 9	

1.3 Correcting errors – voluntary disclosure

If a trader discovers that they have made an error in an earlier VAT return, then they must try to correct it as soon as possible.

There are two methods of correction depending on the size of error:

- inclusion on next VAT return (only if non-deliberate and below threshold – covered later)
- inclusion on Form VAT652 (Notification of Errors in VAT Returns), or by letter.

The information that should be provided HMRC is:

- how the error happened
- the amount of the error
- the VAT period in which it occurred
- whether the error involved input or output tax
- how the error has been calculated
- whether the error is in favour of the business or HMRC.

A taxpayer must use Form VAT652 (or a letter) for larger errors, and where there is a deliberate error, and may use the same form for smaller errors if desired. Taxpayers can even do both, as there is a box on the form that indicates whether the error has been corrected on the return.

Form VAT652 can be downloaded from the HMRC website.

The distinction between a small or large error is determined by the 'error correction reporting threshold'.

The following table explains the threshold limits and summarises which errors can be simply corrected on the next return and which must always be separately disclosed.

Include on next VAT return	Submit on Form VAT652
Errors may be corrected on the next VAT return if they are non-deliberate and: • no more than £10,000; or • between £10,000 and £50,000 but no more than 1% of turnover for the current return period (specifically the 'total sales and other outputs' figure in Box 6 of the VAT).	Errors must be separately disclosed if they: • exceed £50,000; or • exceed £10,000 and are more than 1% of the turnover for the current return period (figure in Box 6 of the return); or • are a deliberate error; or • relate to an accounting period that ended > 4 years ago.

 Test your understanding 2

You are given the following information about the net errors and turnover of four businesses.

For each of them, indicate whether they can correct the error on the next VAT return or whether separate disclosure is required.

Tick ONE box on EACH line.

Assume none of the errors are deliberate and relate to recent accounting periods.

Net error £	Turnover £	Include in VAT return	Separate disclosure
4,500.00	100,000		
12,000.00	250,000		
30,000.00	3,500,000		
60,000.00	10,000,000		

Test your understanding 3

You are given the following information about the non-deliberate net errors and turnover of four businesses.

For each of them, indicate whether they can correct the error on the next VAT return or whether separate disclosure is required.

Tick ONE box on EACH line.

Net error £	Turnover £	Include in VAT return	Separate disclosure
40,000	4,500,000		
55,000	6,000,000		
12,500	300,000		
4,500	40,000		

 Test your understanding 4

Bella is a registered trader who prepares VAT returns quarterly. In the quarter to 30 June 2024, she has a turnover of £103,450 and she discovers the following errors in earlier returns:

1   Bella incorrectly recorded the total of output VAT for the previous quarter as £45,590, when it should have been £54,590.

2   Input VAT on UK customer entertaining of £180, was wrongly reclaimed as input tax in the same quarter.

3   No input tax was reclaimed on the purchase of a computer in September 2023 , costing £1,680 plus VAT.

State the action Bella should take to correct these errors.

 Reference material

Information about correcting errors can be found in the 'Errors in previous VAT Returns' section of your reference material provided in the real assessment, so you do not need to learn it.

Why not look up the correct part of the reference material in the introduction to this text book now?

1.4 Errors found by HMRC

An error may be discovered by HMRC, for example during a VAT control visit. In this case, HMRC may issue a discovery assessment (i.e. a demand) to collect any VAT due.

Normally HMRC have up to four years after the end of the return period in which the error occurred to issue such an assessment.

This is extended to 20 years for errors arising from deliberate behaviour (such as fraud).

HMRC can issue a penalty using the percentages for prompted disclosure in (section 4.1).

 Reference material

Information about errors found by HMRC can be found in the 'Assessments of VAT' section of your reference material provided in the real assessment, so you do not need to learn it.

Why not look up the correct part of the reference material in the introduction to this text book now?

2 Late submission

2.1 Penalty points

There is a penalty points system for late filling of VAT returns. The system is designed to be sympathetic to occasional late payers and be punitive for habitual offenders.

A penalty point is incurred each time a return is submitted late, when the number of points reaches a set level a penalty is applied. The threshold varies depending on how frequently a taxpayer prepares VAT returns.

The thresholds are as follows:

Frequency	Threshold
Annually	2
Quarterly	4

Once the threshold is met, a £200 penalty is charged, this will apply for all subsequent late submissions.

The penalty points are not automatic and HMRC may choose not to apply them if the taxpayer can demonstrate reasonable excuse for the late submission.

Reasonable excuse is not defined and depends on the individual circumstances of the taxpayer but does not include lack of funds or reliance on a third party to submit the return.

 Reference material

Information about late payments can be found in the 'Late submission and late payment of VAT' section of your reference material provided in the real assessment, so you do not need to learn it.

Why not look up the correct part of the reference material in the introduction to this text book now?

 Example

Storm prepares VAT returns quarterly. Prior to 2024 they submitted all VAT returns on time however the recent returns have been submitted as follows:

Quarter ended:	Due date	Submission date
31 March 2024	7 May 2024	10 May 2024
30 June 2024	7 August 2024	18 August 2024
30 September 2024	7 November 2023	10 November 2024
31 December 2024	7 February 2025	19 February 2025
31 March 2025	7 May 2025	7 May 2025
30 June 2025	7 August 2025	10 August 2025

The threshold for quarterly returns is 4.

The fourth late return is for the quarter to 31 December 2024, a penalty of £200 applies in respect of this late return.

The next return is submitted on time and so there is no penalty. Storm stays at the threshold of four penalty points.

The return for the quarter to 30 June 2025 is late and so a further penalty of £200 applies.

2.2 Reset to zero

Individual penalty points expire after two years, provided the taxpayer has not reached the penalty threshold.

Once at the threshold, the points only reset to zero when all the annual returns for the next two years or all the quarterly returns for the next twelve months are submitted on time and all the returns for the last two years have actually been submitted, either on time or late.

 Test your understanding 5

You are given the following information about the VAT returns of Junction Ltd,

Quarter ended	Return submitted
31 Mar 2024	Late
30 Jun 2024	On time
30 Sep 2024	On time
31 Dec 2024	Late
31 Mar 2025	On time
30 Jun 2025	On time
30 Sep 2025	On time
31 Dec 2025	Late
31 Mar 2026	Late

Explain the consequences of any late submissions for Junction Ltd.

3 Late Payment

3.1 Late payment

In addition to submitting a late return there is a further penalty if the payment is also late.

For late payments the penalty is a percentage of the outstanding tax. A first penalty for late payment applies if the payment is more than 15 days overdue, a second penalty for late payment is then applied if the payment is more than 30 days overdue.

Number of days overdue	First late payment penalty	Second late payment penalty
Up to 15 days	None	None
16 – 30 days	2% of VAT outstanding at day 15	None
31 days or more	2% of VAT outstanding at day 15, plus 2% of VAT outstanding at day 30	A daily rate based on 4% per annum charged every day from day 31 until paid in full

If HMRC is satisfied that a taxpayer has a reasonable excuse for paying late then no penalty will be assessed.

The late payment penalty does not apply to taxpayers paying instalments on the annual accounting scheme, the penalties will still apply to the balancing payment due under the scheme.

3.2 Time to pay arrangements

If a taxpayer has difficulty paying the VAT to HMRC they can ask for a Time to Pay arrangement. This is a personalised payment plan agreed by HMRC. A Time to Pay arrangement will prevent subsequent penalties arising. However, if a taxpayer does not keep to the agreed terms of the arrangement the penalties will be applied as if the Time to Pay arrangement never existed.

Example

Jolene pays the VAT for the quarter ended 30 June 2024 on 25 August 2024.

The VAT was due 7 August 2024. The payment is 18 days late and so a penalty of 2% of the outstanding VAT will apply.

If she requested a time to pay arrangement, then no penalty will apply.

3.3 Interest

HMRC will also charge VAT registered businesses late payment interest from the first day the payment is due until it is paid in full. Interest is charged at 2.5% above the Bank of England base rate. For example, if base rate is 5%, the rate of interest charged is 7.5%.

The interest is charged on the outstanding VAT and any late paid penalties. Penalties are due to be paid within 30 days of notification.

Late payment interest will continue to accrue on late paid amounts, even if they are included in a Time to Pay arrangement.

Where tax is overpaid, HMRC will pay repayment interest on any tax due to be repaid. This will be paid from either the last day the payment was due to be received or the day it was received (whichever is later) until the date of repayment. The rate will be paid at the Bank of England base rate less 1% (with a minimum of 0.5%). For example, if base rate is 5% the rate of interest is 4%.

Interest for late payment does not apply to tax payers paying instalments on the annual accounting scheme, the interest will however still apply to the balancing payment due under the scheme.

 Reference material

Information about late payments and interest and interest can be found in the 'Late submission and late payment of VAT' section of your reference material provided in the real assessment, so you do not need to learn it.

Example

Rayne's VAT return for the quarter ended 30 June 2024, was submitted late, and the VAT due of £14,500 was not paid until 16 September 2024. This was the first quarter in which they were late submitting and paying the VAT.

This is the first **late submission** and so a penalty point is awarded to Rayne. There is no penalty for late submission as the threshold of 4 points has not been reached.

The return is paid late and so there will be a **late payment** penalty. The payment was due on the 7 August 2024. The number of days the payment is overdue is 40 days.

Interest is charged daily from 8 August to 16 September inclusive.

The first penalty is 2% of the VAT owed after 15 days so £290 (£14,500 × 2%).

A further penalty of 2% (£290) is due because the VAT is not paid within 30 days.

Finally, a daily rate is applied as the VAT had not been paid for over 30 days.

4% × £14,500 × 10/365 = £15.89

The total penalty for late payment is £885.89 (£290 + £290 + £15.89).

Finally, **interest** will be due on the late payment. Assuming that the bank base rate is 5%.

5% + 2.5% = 7.5% interest is charged on the amount outstanding, calculated daily.

£14,500 × 7.5% × 40/365 = £119.18

Test your understanding 6

1 HMRC issue an assessment on 30 June 2025 showing £3,200 VAT payable, for the quarter ended 31 July 2024. Take Ltd paid the outstanding sum on 7 July 2025.

  Calculate the interest charged on a daily basis, assume the Bank of England base rate is 5%.

2 Which one of the following is the most accurate statement of the consequence of submitting an incorrect VAT return?

  A A penalty may be charged and the error must be corrected on the next VAT return

  B A penalty may be charged and the error must be corrected by submitting it on Form VAT 652

  C A penalty will be charged and the way in which the error is corrected depends on its size

  D A penalty may be charged and the way in which the error is corrected depends on its size

3 Tariq finds that he made a non-deliberate net error on an earlier VAT return of £12,400.00. If his turnover for the current quarter is £750,000, how should he correct the error?

  A By inclusion on his next VAT return

  B By separate notification on Form VAT 652 or by letter

4 Further penalties

4.1 Standardised penalties

HMRC has a standardised penalty regime that applies to a range of taxes including VAT.

In addition to late filing and payment penalties, a trader can be penalised for failing to register by the compulsory registration due date, or for submitting an inaccurate VAT return

A penalty may be charged if the error is careless or deliberate. The penalty is a percentage of the net error.

Type of behaviour	Unprompted disclosure	Prompted disclosure
Careless	0 – 30%	15 – 30%
Deliberate	20 – 70%	35 – 70%
Deliberate and concealed	30 – 100%	50 – 100%

If a trader discovers a non-careless accidental error, such as a simple mistake, then they must take steps to correct it. If they do not, then HMRC will treat it as a careless error and a penalty may be charged.

Generally, the penalty charged for a careless error is lower than the maximum possible, unless there has been a sequence of careless errors.

 Example

Sharleen is a VAT registered trader. She deliberately increased the input tax she reclaimed on her VAT return for the quarter ended 30 September 2024 by submitting fake expense invoices worth £1,000. During a control visit HMRC discovers the error and issues a discovery assessment to collect the £200 of VAT due (£1,000 × 20%).

As the error is deliberate and concealed and the disclosure was prompted (by the control visit) the minimum penalty for the error is £200 × 50% = £100 and the maximum penalty for the error is £200 × 100% = £200.

Example

Lemond is a registered trader who prepares VAT returns quarterly. He discovers that in his previous quarter he entered VAT output tax on his return as £56,792.00 when it should have been £65,972.00. He also entered input tax as £45,510.00 when it should have been £45,150.00.

He also discovers that he has not reclaimed the VAT of £3,450.00 on the purchase of a new milling machine.

The net VAT error is calculated as

	£
Output tax understated (£65,972.00 – £56,792.00)	9,180.00
Input tax overstated (£45,510.00 – £45,150.00)	360.00
Input tax understated – not claimed on machine	(3,450.00)
	_____
Net VAT error (extra VAT due)	6,090.00
	_____

If Lemond discovered the error and made an immediate effort to correct it right away this is likely to be viewed by HMRC as a careless error. The maximum penalty would be 30% of the net VAT error = £1,827 (30% × £6,090).

 Reference material

Information about penalties for errors in returns can be found in the 'Penalties for inaccuracies in VAT return' section of your reference material provided in the real assessment, so you do not need to learn it.

Why not look up the correct part of the reference material in the introduction to this text book now?

4.2 Failure to register

If a trader does not register for VAT when the business's turnover goes over the compulsory registration threshold, there are two consequences.

(i) All the VAT that the trader **should have charged** from the date they **should have registered** is payable to HMRC. The trader is most likely to treat the relevant sales as VAT-inclusive and suffer the cost of the VAT themselves.

(ii) A penalty can be charged, which is a percentage of the VAT due, known as the potential lost revenue (PLR). The amount of the penalty depends on whether the trader deliberately failed to register, when the trader informed HMRC of the need to register, and whether the disclosure of the need to register was prompted or unprompted.

Type of behaviour	Within 12 months of tax being due		12 months or more after tax was due	
	unprompted	prompted	unprompted	prompted
Non-deliberate	0 – 30%	10 – 30%	10 – 30%	20 – 30%

Type of behaviour	Unprompted	Prompted
Deliberate	20 – 70%	35 – 70%
Deliberate and concealed	30 – 100%	50 – 100%

 Example

Beverley runs a business manufacturing silicon cookware, which is a standard-rated supply.

On 1 October 2024, whilst talking to a friend, she realises she should have been registered since 1 March 2024 and immediately contacts HMRC. Her turnover since that date is £27,000 and she has suffered input VAT of £3,000 in that time.

The invoices will normally be treated as VAT-inclusive, so she will have to pay VAT to HMRC of £1,500 ((20/120 × £27,000) – £3,000).

As Beverley does not appear to have deliberately failed to register for VAT, and made an unprompted disclosure to HMRC within 12 months of the date she should have registered the minimum penalty will be £0 and the maximum will be 30% × £1,500 = £450.

4.3 Other penalties

If a trader does not submit any VAT return at all, then HMRC can issue an assessment that estimates the amount of VAT due. If this estimate is too low and the trader does not tell HMRC within 30 days that it is too low, then a penalty can be charged for that omission too.

A penalty can be charge at 30% of the potential lost revenue.

A maximum penalty of up to £500 may be charged for each failure to retain adequate records in respect of a VAT return for the prescribed period (six years).

4.4 Reasonable excuse

None of the penalties in this chapter will be applied if there is a reasonable excuse. There is no legal definition of reasonable excuse but if the trader shows that his or her conduct was that of a conscientious business person who wished to comply with VAT requirements, there may be a reasonable excuse for example where the trader:

- has suffered the bereavement of a life partner or close relative

- has had a serious illness (or his or her life partner or close relative has had a serious illness)

- has written evidence that there is doubt over the liability of the supply to VAT.

Note that inability to pay the VAT due is not a reasonable excuse.

 Reference material

Information about penalties for late registration can be found in the 'Failure to register for VAT' section of your reference material provided in the real assessment, so you do not need to learn it.

Why not look up the correct part of the reference material in the introduction to this text book now?

Test your understanding 7

Indicate whether the following statements about VAT errors and penalties are true or false.

Tick one box on each line

		True	False
1	If a trader fails to register at the correct time, the business will have to pay HMRC all the VAT that should have charged to customers since the date the business should have been registered.		
2	If a trader makes an error in a VAT return, the trader will always be charged a penalty.		
3	A penalty only occurs if a trader both pays VAT late and submits a VAT return late.		
4	Interest for late payment of VAT is at 2.5% above the Bank of England base rate.		

5 Communicating VAT information

5.1 Advising managers of the impact of VAT payments

Once the return has been completed, it must be submitted to HMRC and any VAT owing paid over to HMRC. As discussed previously the submission and payment are completed electronically.

In your assessment, you may be asked to complete a short email to the financial accountant or another manager, giving the details of the return submission and the amount payable or receivable.

It will be important for the financial accountant (or other person responsible for managing the cash payments of the business) to know when the payment will be made, so that they can make sure that the funds are available in the bank account at the correct time.

You may be required to complete something similar to this:

 Example

To: Financial Accountant
From: Dawn Jones
Date: 17 April 2024
Subject: VAT return

I have completed the draft VAT return for the quarter ended 31 March 2024.

The amount of VAT payable will be £3,561.42.

This will be paid electronically by 7 May 2024.

If you need any further information, please contact me.

Best wishes

Dawn (Junior Accountant)

This task in the exam will not be a free entry question. Instead, a partly complete piece of communication will be provided which needs to be completed, by way of drop down boxes, date pickers and number boxes.

5.2   Ethical implications

It is important to adhere to the AAT's Professional Code of Ethics. Advising managers of correct payment dates demonstrates professional competence and due care.

Members must act with integrity and resist any pressure to omit transactions or falsify dates.

VAT can be complicated, particularly when dealing with overseas transactions. If asked for information that is beyond your level of knowledge or experience, you should refer queries to your line manager.

Test your understanding 8

You are an accounting technician for a business.

You are preparing the VAT return for the quarter ended 30 June 2024. In this quarter, the business spent £2,400, including VAT, on a party for the 20 staff who all brought a guest.

Your supervisor has asked you to reclaim all the VAT on the cost of the party as in their words 'no one at HMRC will know if there were guests at the party or not'.

Which of the following is your correct response?

A   You do as your supervisor asks as it is their responsibility if VAT rules are broken.

B   You do as your supervisor asks but make a note in the file that you have done so.

C   You tell your supervisor that you cannot do as they ask, as it is both a breach of VAT rules and your AAT Professional Code of Ethics.

6 Summary

The penalties for VAT errors can be summarised as follows.

Error/omissions	Action
Failing to register	HMRC can issue an assessment to collect tax due and charge a penalty.
Failure to submit a return	HMRC can issue an assessment to collect tax due.
Failure to tell HMRC that an estimated VAT assessment is too low, within 30 days	HMRC can charge a penalty.
Making a non-careless error	Must take steps to correct otherwise error may be regarded as careless.
Making a careless or deliberate error	Trader must correct the error. HMRC can also charge a penalty.
Correcting errors	Inclusion on Form VAT 652 or by letter. If below limit, can simply include the correction on next return
Errors found by HMRC	HMRC can raise an assessment within 4 years of the end of the VAT period (careless errors) or 20 years (deliberate errors, including fraud). A penalty can be charged.
Submitting a VAT return late or paying VAT late	Penalty regime applies.
Failure to disclose business changes	HMRC can charge a penalty.

Test your understanding answers

Test your understanding 1

		£
VAT due sales and other outputs	Box 1	4,324.00
VAT due on acquisitions of goods made in Northern Ireland from EU Member States	Box 2	0.00
Total VAT due (the sum of boxes 1 and 2)	Box 3	4,324.00
VAT reclaimed on purchases and other inputs, (including acquisitions in Northern Ireland from EU Member States)	Box 4	1,835.12
Net VAT to be paid to HMRC (Difference between boxes 3 and 4)	Box 5	2,488.88
Total value of sales and all other outputs excluding any VAT.	Box 6	22,020
Total value of purchases and all other inputs excluding any VAT.	Box 7	9,176
Total value of dispatches of goods and related costs, excluding any VAT, from Northern Ireland to EU Member States	Box 8	0
Total value of acquisitions of goods and related costs, excluding any VAT, made in Northern Ireland from EU Member States	Box 9	0

Workings for VAT return

		£
Box 1:	From VAT account	4,300.00
	Error on previous return	24.00
		4,324.00

Note that the output VAT total of £4,324.00 is not 20% of sales in the sales account of £22,020. This is because the sales figure is likely to be a mix of standard-rated plus zero-rated or exempt sales.

		£
Box 4:	From VAT account	1,820.00
	Petty cash	15.12
		1,835.12

		£
Box 7:	From Purchases account	9,100
	Petty cash (£75.60 rounded to the nearest pound)	76
		9,176

Test your understanding 2

1   Error £4,500.00 – include on VAT return as below £10,000

2   Error £12,000.00 – separate disclosure is needed as this error is more than £10,000 and is more than 1% of turnover

3   Error £30,000.00 – can be included on VAT return as between £10,000 and £50,000 and less than 1% of turnover

4   Error £60,000.00 – must be separately disclosed as more than £50,000

💧 Test your understanding 3

1 Include in VAT return.

The error is between £10,000 and £50,000 and less than 1% of turnover.

2 Separate disclosure. The error is more than £50,000.

3 Separate disclosure.

The error is over £10,000 and more than 1% of turnover.

4 Include in VAT return. The error is less than £10,000.

✳ Test your understanding 4

		£
1 Output VAT	(£54,590 – £45,590)	9,000
2 UK customer entertaining		180
3 Computer input VAT	(£1,680 × 20%)	(336)
		8,844

De minimis limit = greater of:

(i) £10,000

(ii) (1% × £103,450) = £1,034

As the net error of £8,844 is below the de minimis limit of £10,000 Bella should include the amounts on her return to 30 June 2024.

This increases her VAT payable for the quarter ended 30 June 2024 by £8,844.

Test your understanding 5

You are given the following information about the VAT returns of Junction Ltd,

Quarter ended	Return submitted
31 Mar 2024	Late
30 Jun 2024	On time
30 Sep 2024	On time
31 Dec 2024	Late
31 Mar 2025	On time
30 Jun 2025	On time
30 Sep 2025	On time
31 Dec 2025	Late
31 Mar 2026	Late

Explain the consequences of any late payments for Junction Ltd.

No penalty arises for the first three late returns.

A point is awarded for each late return.

The penalty points after the 31 December 2025 return are three, no penalty applies to this or previous late returns as the threshold of 4 has not been reached.

The first penalty point (31 March 2024) expires after two years and so the threshold after the 31 March 2026 return will continue to be three (December 2024, December 2025 and March 2026).

The threshold of 4 penalty points has not been reached and so no penalty arises.

Test your understanding 6

1   Interest runs from 8 September 2024 to 7 July 2025. Default interest of £3,200 × 7.5% (2.5% + 5%) × (23 + 31 + 30 + 31 + 31 + 28 + 31 + 30 + 31 + 30 + 7)/365 = £199.23 will be charged.

2   The correct answer is D.

     Whether or not a penalty is charged depends on the circumstances.

3   The correct answer is B.

     The error is between £10,000 and £50,000 but is more than 1% of turnover, hence it must be separately disclosed.

 Test your understanding 7

1   True

2   False – whether or not a penalty is charged depends on the circumstances.

3   False – these are two separate offences and are dealt with separately. It does not therefore have to be both.

4   True

 Test your understanding 8

The correct answer is C.

It is important that you can demonstrate integrity and professional behaviour and are not swayed by pressure to act illegally and allow irrecoverable VAT to appear in the VAT return.

Employer responsibilities for payroll

Introduction

This chapter looks at an employer's payroll responsibilities, including registering with HMRC, keeping records, and making deductions from gross pay.

It is important for employers to be aware of the responsibilities so that they don't incur penalties for non-compliance.

ASSESSMENT CRITERIA	CONTENTS
Employer responsibilities of payroll (4.1)	1 Employing staff 2 Records 3 Deductions from pay

1 Employing staff

1.1 Introduction to PAYE

Businesses or individuals who take on staff become employers. They operate payroll to pay these employees, usually with regular paydays such as each month or each week.

Employers have legal responsibilities to HMRC, the relevant tax authority, for their payroll operations.

Employees are charged income tax and national insurance contributions (NICs) on the salaries or wages they receive for doing their jobs.

When paying an employee each payday, the employer must deduct (hold back) an amount for the employee's income tax and NICs. The employee receives only the net amount after these deductions.

The employer pays the deductions of tax and NICs directly to HMRC. In this way, the employer acts as a collector of the amounts due to HMRC from employees.

The system by which deductions of income tax are made in this way is referred to as the Pay As You Earn (PAYE) system, and the income tax is known as PAYE.

The employee's NICs also deducted are known as Class 1 primary contributions. The employer is also charged NICs on the salaries and wages paid to employees. These NICs suffered by the employer are known as Class 1 secondary contributions. Both sets of NICs are paid to HMRC with PAYE.

Rules for reporting and paying PAYE and NICs are covered in Chapter 9.

 Definition

Pay As You Earn (PAYE) is the name given to the system under which employers deduct income tax from the wages and salaries that they pay their employees. The income tax deducted is itself referred to as PAYE.

Class 1 National Insurance Contributions (NICs) are suffered by employees (primary contributions) and employers (secondary contributions) on the wages and salaries of employees. They are paid to HMRC along with PAYE.

Example

Kat employs John, with a weekly wage of £400 (gross). Kat deducts PAYE and employee's NICs of £44 per week so John receives £356 (£400 – £44) each payday.

Kat pays employer's NICs in respect of John of £31 per week and so pays a total of £75 (£44 + £31) to HMRC.

To work out how much PAYE and NICs to deduct, and the employer's NICs, the employer needs information about the employee including the tax code that HMRC have issued to the employee.

 Definition

A **tax code** is provided by HMRC for each employee each tax year. For this assessment you do not need to know how the tax code is worked out or how it is used to calculate deductions.

The **tax year** runs from 6 April in one year to 5 April in the next year.

We will cover, in more detail, pay and deductions later in this chapter. There are other deductions which may be made from an employee's pay. Some of these (like PAYE and NICs) must be made by law. Others are deducted either because the employer is entitled to make the deduction, or because the employee chooses for the deduction to be made.

As the employer is responsible for making the tax deductions, it follows that there are strict rules regarding an employer's operation of payroll. These include registering as an employer and keeping records, which are covered in this chapter. In Chapter 9 there are other obligations concerned with reporting information and paying PAYE and NICs to HMRC.

An employer may pay an external payroll provider, such as a payroll bureau or an accountant to operate payroll on its behalf. However, the employer remains responsible for compliance with the rules.

1.2 Registering as an employer

Businesses or individuals must register with HMRC as an employer when it starts employing staff.

Strictly, an employer must register if any of the following applies to any employee:

- is paid £123 or more per week

- has another job

- receives a pension

- is provided with benefits by the employer.

This means most employers must register. Even if they do not have to register, employers must keep certain records and provide payslips – payslips are covered in Chapter 9.

Most businesses will register online. Although most employers will be businesses, private individuals may also employ staff e.g. personal assistants, carers or housekeepers working in their homes, and must also register as employers. Such employers may need to telephone HMRC to register.

An employer must register before the first payday and cannot register more than two months before starting to pay employees.

Reference material

Information about the time frame for registering as an employer can be found in the 'Payroll deadlines' section of your reference material provided in the real assessment.

Why not look up the correct part of the reference material in the introduction to this text book now?

Example

Tariq is a sole trader. He wants to employ Lisa, his first employee, from 1 June. Lisa will be paid £20,000 per annum, and she will be paid on 25th of each month.

Tariq must register with HMRC as an employer before 25 June, the first payday. He cannot register before 25 April, two months before the first payday.

1.3 Employment allowance

Employers receive an allowance to reduce the total employer's class 1 NIC (i.e. secondary) liability. The employment allowance for the tax year 2024/25 is £5,000 per annum per employer (not per person).

- If the employer's liability is less than the allowance the employer pays no class 1 employer's NIC's for the year.

- The allowance cannot be used against other classes of NIC's e.g. Class 1A

The employment allowance is not available to:

- Companies where a director is the sole employee

- Employers with total class 1 employer's NIC ≥ £100,000 in the previous tax year (the previous year's NIC liability will be provided in questions where required).

After an employer has registered, HMRC will issue an employer PAYE reference number (ERN) which is used on payroll records, and an Accounts Office reference used when making payments.

An employer who fails to register will be liable to penalties for failure to report employee payments to HMRC and failure to pay PAYE and NICs to HMRC. These penalties are covered in Chapter 9.

 Test your understanding 1

Which one of the following is not true about registering as an employer with HMRC?

A   An employer can register up to two months before paying its first employee.

B   An individual must run a business to be able to register.

C   An employer must register to receive an employer PAYE reference.

D   An employer using a payroll bureau must still be registered.

---

2 Records

2.1 Records

An employer must keep records relating to employees for many reasons, including to comply with employment law. There are specific payroll records which an employer must keep in order to comply with tax law.

Such records include documents and worksheets of supporting calculations, which relate to:

- employees' pay before deductions
- PAYE deductions
- NICs, both deducted and suffered by the employer
- other deductions made from pay (section 3)
- taxable benefits given to employees (Chapter 9).

Details of reports and payments made to HMRC must be kept for three years from the end of the tax year to which they relate. HMRC can issue a penalty of £3,000 if an employer fails to keep proper records.

 Reference material

> The reference material provided in the real assessment gives the retention period for records and the penalty for failure to maintain records in the section 'Payroll record retention'.
>
> Why not look up the correct part of the reference material in the introduction to this text book now?

Most of these records will be kept digitally as the employer uses software to operate payroll. However, some documents may be in paper form, such as those used when an employee starts or leaves a business. These must also be retained.

2.2 Software

An employer must usually report payroll information to HMRC online. The employer therefore needs payroll software. Using software should also make payroll easier to manage, especially for large numbers of employees.

Employers with fewer than ten employees can use free payroll software provided by HMRC or commercial suppliers. HMRC's own free software is called Basic PAYE Tools. An employer must be registered with HMRC and have a login for HMRC's PAYE Online service, before being able to use Basic PAYE Tools.

Employers with ten or more employees must purchase software. HMRC tests payroll software and lists products which it recognises on the GOV.UK website.

Whether using free or paid-for software, the employer needs to check that the software has all the functions it needs to operate payroll. The operation of payroll is covered in Chapter 9 in more detail.

The employer should regularly back-up software to ensure the appropriate records are retained.

The calculations of PAYE and NICs depend on tax rates, allowances and limits which are set by legislation and which often change each tax year. Software providers usually update their software to reflect these changes on a timely basis. Therefore, employers must make sure they read and follow any instructions and information received from their software provider. They should run the appropriate software updates and make sure their software reflects the correct tax year.

3 Deductions from pay

3.1 Types of pay

Gross pay is the total amount payable to the employee before any deductions are made.

Gross pay can be made up of many different elements including basic pay, overtime payments and bonuses. The basic pay may be a salary (a fixed amount usually quoted annually e.g. £30,000 p.a.) or wages, which are calculated by multiplying the pay rate by the time worked in the pay period (e.g. £10 per hour for the number of hours worked in the month).

As covered earlier, the employer must make various deductions from gross pay, so that the employee receives a lower amount known as net pay.

Employees are charged income tax and NICs on their pay. Usually the full amount of gross pay is taxable, so that the taxable pay is the same as gross pay.

However, some deductions can reduce the amount of the gross pay which is chargeable to income tax. In this case the amount of pay on which tax is charged (taxable pay) is less than gross pay.

 Definition

Pay rate is the amount of money employees are paid per hour, per week or per item made.

Gross pay is the total amount payable to an employee before any deductions are made.

Net pay is the total amount received by an employee after all deductions have been made.

Taxable pay is the amount of gross pay which is chargeable to income tax.

3.2 Statutory deductions

The main deductions are PAYE and NICs. These must be made by law and are known as statutory deductions. The deductions are recorded and paid over to HMRC – details are given in Chapter 9.

There are other statutory deductions such as those relating to student loans. If the employee had previously taken out certain student or postgraduate loans to pay for higher education, the employer must make deductions from the employee's pay in order to repay the loans. The deductions are paid over to HMRC with the PAYE and NICs.

3.3 Pension contributions

A common deduction is for pension contributions. To increase pension saving, the UK government requires employers to enrol most employees automatically into a pension scheme. Both the employer and the employee then make contributions to the scheme, usually based on a percentage of basic salary. There is a minimum percentage that the employer must contribute and a minimum percentage that must be contributed by the employee and employer in total.

Employees do have the right to 'opt out' of the scheme if they so wish but then they lose out on the employer contributions too.

Definition

Employee pension contributions are deductions from pay that contribute to the employee's pension scheme.

The contributions by the employer are not taxable on the employee. They do not form part of gross or taxable pay.

The treatment of the employee's contributions depends on the particular pension arrangement used. The arrangement covered here is a 'net pay' arrangement used to make contributions to an occupational pension scheme of the employer.

Under the net pay arrangement, the employer deducts the employee's pension contribution from gross pay when operating payroll. The employer pays the pension contribution over to the pension scheme.

The employee's contribution decreases the taxable pay of the employee i.e. the employee suffers less PAYE (income tax) because of the contribution. This tax relief is given to encourage individuals to save more, but applies to income tax only, not NIC.

Example

Devi is an employee of Gravel Ltd and has a salary is £24,000 p.a. Gravel Ltd makes an employer pension contribution for Devi of £100 per month. Devi also contributes £150 per month to the pension scheme under a net pay arrangement.

Gravel Ltd's contribution of £100 is not included in Devi's gross pay or taxable pay i.e. her gross pay is £24,000/12 = £2,000 per month.

Devi's taxable pay is £1,850 (£2,000 – £150) per month, so Gravel Ltd calculates PAYE on this amount.

Both Devi's primary and Gravel Ltd's secondary class 1 NICs are calculated on the gross pay amount of £2,000.

Devi receives net pay of £1,850 less the PAYE and employee's NIC.

Gravel Ltd pays the total of £250 (£100 + £150) to the pension scheme and also the PAYE and NICs to HMRC.

3.4 Non-statutory deductions

Employers **must** make the deductions described above.

Employers may also be **entitled** to make other deductions from pay. For example, an employer may correct a previous overpayment of wages by a deduction on a later payday, within certain rules.

In some sectors, till shortfalls, breakages, or failures by customers to pay may be made up by deductions from employees' pay. An example is deductions from the wages of waiting staff in a restaurant if a customer leaves without paying. However, employment law provides some protections. For an employer to make the deduction, there must be a prior written agreement in place, which may be part of the employment contract.

Employees may also **choose** for other deductions to be made. These are known as voluntary deductions.

Examples of voluntary deductions include:

- Union membership fees - certain trade union subscriptions are deducted directly from an employee's pay and paid over to the trade union by the employing business. This is known as paying by "check-off" but cannot be done without the employee's written consent.

- Private medical insurance – generally such schemes are funded by employer contributions but sometimes the employee will also be required to contribute with those amounts being deducted from the employee's pay.

- Savings schemes established by employers for their employees. These enable employees to make regular savings by having the amounts they wish to save on a regular basis deducted directly from their pay and paid into the relevant savings scheme.

Most voluntary deductions do not have an effect on taxable pay i.e. the deduction is made after PAYE and NICs have been calculated and deducted.

Such deductions may not be made without the written authorisation of the employee, or inclusion in the individual's contract of employment.

3.5 Charitable giving

A common voluntary deduction which does reduce taxable pay, and so affects PAYE, is charitable giving.

 Definition

Charitable giving is a scheme under which employees can make contributions to charity. It is also known as the payroll giving scheme or **GAYE (Give As You Earn)**.

To encourage people to give to charity, the government allows the charitable deduction to be made before the PAYE is calculated and paid, i.e. taxable pay is reduced. However, there is no reduction in NICs which are calculated before the deduction is made.

The employee instructs the employer to make regular deductions from the employee's gross pay. The deductions are then paid over to an approved agency. The agency will make donations to various charities in accordance with the employee's instructions.

There are no statutory requirements as to the format of records to be kept, but the employer must keep the employee's authorisation and records of deductions made for the usual period of at least three years.

Test your understanding 2

Fill in the blanks in the following statements from the picklist that follows.

The amount of pay received by an employee after all deductions have been made is the employee's .... pay.

An employer calculates PAYE on an employee's .... pay.

The total of an employee's pay including wages and overtime, before deduction of PAYE and NICs, is the employee's .... pay.

Picklist: gross   net   taxable

 Test your understanding 3

Indicate whether the following statements about different payroll deductions are true or false.

Tick one box on each line.

		True	False
1	Charitable giving is a statutory deduction that must be made.		
2	Employee pension contributions reduce the tax liability of the employee.		
3	Charitable giving deductions have no effect on PAYE and NICs.		
4	Student loan deductions have no effect on NICs payable.		
5	Gross pay is less than taxable pay if the employee makes net pay pension contributions.		

Test your understanding 4

Indicate whether authorisation by the employee is or is not required before the following deductions can be made.

Tick one box on each line.

	Authorisation required	Authorisation not required
PAYE, NICs and student loan deductions		
Voluntary deductions such as charitable giving payments		
Deductions set out in a contract of employment		

4 Summary

In this chapter, we have considered the financial implications of employing somene as a member of staff.

A business, whether employing just 1 or many members of staff is required to operate a payroll system, register with HMRC, keep accurate records and make the relevant deductions from the employees gross pay to arrive at net pay.

Calculation of net pay

	£	£
Gross pay		
Basic pay (salary or wages)		X
Additional pay (e.g. overtime, bonuses)		X
Deductions		
Statutory deductions:		
PAYE (i.e. income tax)	X	
Employee's NICs	X	
Student loan repayments	X	
Employee pension contributions (unless opted out)	X	
Voluntary deductions:		
Charitable giving	X	
	___	
Total deductions		(X)
		___
Net pay		X
		___

KAPLAN PUBLISHING

Test your understanding answers

Test your understanding 1

The correct answer is B.

An individual employing someone such as a carer or to work in his, her or their home must also register as an employer.

Test your understanding 2

The amount of pay received by an employee after all deductions have been made is the employee's **net** pay.

An employer calculates PAYE on an employee's **taxable** pay.

The total of an employee's pay including wages and overtime, before deduction of PAYE and NICs, is the employee's **gross** pay.

Test your understanding 3

1   False – charitable giving is a voluntary deduction.

2   True – employee pension contributions reduce taxable pay if made under a net payment arrangement. They do not reduce NICs. Employer pension contributions are not part of taxable pay.

3   False – charitable giving deductions are deducted to give taxable pay, before PAYE is calculated, but they do not reduce NICs.

4   True – student loan deductions are deductions with no effect on PAYE or NICs.

5   False – taxable pay is lower than gross pay, by the amount of the employee pension contributions.

Test your understanding 4

Authorisation from the employee is required for voluntary deductions such as charitable giving payments, but not for PAYE, NICs, student loan deductions or deductions set out in a contract of employment.

Operating payroll

Introduction

This chapter looks at the forms produced for payroll, the reporting and payment obligations of employers to HMRC, and possible penalties.

It also covers the communication of payroll information within an organisation and HMRC powers in relation to payroll.

ASSESSMENT CRITERIA	CONTENTS
Operating payroll (4.2)	1 Payroll reporting
Communicating information on payroll related matters (5.1)	2 Full Payment Submission (FPS)
Legislation, regulation, guidance and codes of practice (5.2)	3 Employer Payment Summary (EPS)
	4 Payments to HMRC
	5 Year-end reporting
	6 Penalties
	7 Communicating payroll information

1 Payroll reporting

1.1 Payslips

When employers operate payroll, they have responsibilities to report information to HMRC but also to their employees.

Employees have a legal right to a payslip which shows how their pay has been worked out. This must be given to the employee on or before each payday, for that pay period.

The payslip will include the names of the employer and the employee, and the date of payment.

It must show, for that pay period:

- gross pay

- number of hours paid where pay depends on hours worked.

- deductions including PAYE and national insurance contributions (NICs), student loan deductions, pension contributions, and voluntary deductions

- net pay after these deductions

The payslip may also show the totals of these amounts for the tax year to date.

An employer may choose to detail fixed deductions, which do not vary in amount over time, in a separate written statement.

It is also the choice of the employer whether to provide the payslip in a printed or electronic (online) format.

Information about the employee might include the tax code and national insurance number (NINO) issued to the employee by HMRC.

 Definition

Each individual in the UK is issued with a **national insurance number (NINO)**. The purpose of the NINO is to make sure each person's national insurance contributions and tax are recorded against that individuals name only.

1.2 Real Time Information (RTI)

Employers have responsibilities to report information about employee pay to HMRC. Some reports are required after the end of the tax year, and these are covered later in this chapter. Remember that a tax year runs from 6 April in one year to 5 April in the next.

The ongoing reporting of pay to HMRC during the tax year takes place under a system called the Real Time Information (RTI) system.

 Definition

Real Time Information (RTI) refers to the system which requires an employer to submit payroll information to HMRC on or before each payday, rather than after the event.

Given the real time nature of the reporting system, employers must be organised in the operation of payroll. Previously in Chapter 8 we learnt software is used to operate payroll which can then be used to submit the reports online.

Details of the reports required in respect of each payday are covered in the next sections.

2 Full Payment Submission (FPS)

2.1 What is the FPS?

Each time an employer pays an employee, the employer must submit a Full Payment Submission (FPS) to HMRC's PAYE Online service. The FPS is both completed and submitted via the employer's payroll software.

Under RTI, the FPS must be submitted on or before the date the employees are paid.

 Definition

Full Payment Submission (FPS) is an electronic report submitted on or before each payday to notify HMRC of payments to employees and deductions made.

2.2 Content of the FPS

The FPS contains information about the employer, the employees, and their pay and deductions. An FPS is also used to report information regarding new starters and leaving employees.

Employer information includes:

- HMRC office number
- Employer PAYE reference
- Accounts Office reference
- the relevant tax year.

Information for each employee includes:

- NINO
- title and name
- date of birth
- gender
- address – if this has changed, or if the employee is new, or if NINO is not known
- payroll ID – a reference which may be assigned by the employer to each employee
- tax code
- indicator of hours normally worked.

Pay and deductions information for each employee for the period i.e. the month or week covered by the FPS, includes:

- taxable pay and pay subject to NICs
- PAYE and NICs deducted or refunded
- student loan deductions
- pay after these deductions
- employee pension contributions
- other deductions made from pay
- employer's NICs.

Totals must also be included for most of these amounts for the tax year to date on a cumulative basis.

Additional information includes pay frequency, payment date, and the tax week or month number in the tax year to which this FPS refers.

Definition

A **tax month** runs from 6th of one month to 5th of the next.

The FPS is also used to report information of starters and leavers.

Reference material

The reference material provided in the real assessment gives the timing for submission of the FPS in the section 'Types of payroll submission'. This section also gives a one-line summary of what is entered on the FPS, but does not give the detail of the lists above.

Why not look up the correct part of the reference material in the introduction to this text book now?

Test your understanding 1

Indicate whether the following statements about the FPS are true or false.

Tick one box on each line.

		True	False
1	The FPS includes details of how long the employee has worked for the employer.		
2	The employer gives each employee an FPS each payday.		
3	The FPS shows the amount of each employee's pay and deductions for the pay period.		

2.3 Starters

When a new employee starts work, the employer must gather information in order to add the employee to the payroll and make the correct deductions.

The employee may provide the employer with a copy of a form P45, given to the employee on leaving a previous employment. Details of the P45 are covered later in this chapter. Otherwise, the employee completes a form known as a new starter checklist.

The information from the P45 or from a declaration on the checklist allows the employer to determine the tax code for the employee, so that the correct PAYE deductions will be made. The forms contain other information such as whether student loan deductions must be made.

 Definition

New starter checklist is a form completed by a new employee if they do not have a recent P45. The checklist enables the employer to add the starter to the payroll and make the correct deductions from pay.

The employer registers the new employee with HMRC by including the employee's details on the FPS the first time the new employee is paid.

On the FPS, the employer enters the employee's start date and the starter declaration, and indicates if student loan deductions are required. The employer completes the usual employee information required on an FPS, as well as entering the employee's passport number if this was collected. Details of pay and deductions are given for the new employment only.

2.4 Leavers and form P45

When an employee leaves, the employer puts the date of leaving on the FPS of the employee's final payment.

The employer must also give the employee a form P45 completed using the employer's payroll software. The employee keeps one part of the form (1A) for his or her own records. The employee then gives Parts 2 and 3 to his or her new employer.

The P45 gives:

- the employer PAYE reference

- employee details such as name, address, NINO etc.

- the leaving date

- the tax code at the leaving date

- whether student loan deductions are made

- the total pay and tax deducted from the start of the tax year until the leaving date.

 Definition

P45 is a form given by an employer to a leaving employee, recording pay and tax deducted for the tax year to date and other information enabling the employee's new employer to make the correct deductions.

Test your understanding 2

Indicate whether the following statements about the procedures when an employee leaves employment are true or false.

Tick one box on each line.

		True	False
1	The employee gives the employer a P45 as proof of resignation.		
2	The P45 states the employee's home address.		
3	The employer notifies HMRC of the employee's leaving date on the FPS.		

Test your understanding 3

Twigg Ltd pays employees on 25 August for their work for the month of August. Twigg Ltd takes on a new employee Jane from 1 September and asks for her P45 form from her previous employment.

1   By what date must the FPS for the 25 August payday be submitted?

    A   25 August

    B   31 August

    C   1 September

    D   5 September

2   What information would not be given on Jane's P45?

    A   Confirmation of Jane's right to work in the UK.

    B   Whether student loan deductions are made.

    C   Jane's tax code when she left her previous job.

    D   Jane's pay for the tax year to date.

3   Which of the following statements regarding Jane's first payday is false?

    A   Jane will receive a payslip showing pay and deductions.

    B   Twigg Ltd will include Jane's start date on the FPS.

    C   Jane's P45 will be updated to include her new pay.

    D   Twigg Ltd will deduct PAYE and NICs from Jane's gross pay.

3   Employer Payment Summary (EPS)

3.1   What is the EPS used for?

An Employer Payment Summary (EPS) is submitted in certain circumstances. An example of when an EPS is used instead of an FPS is if an employer has not paid any employees in a tax month.

The EPS must then be submitted by the 19th of the tax month following the tax month in which no employees were paid.

As for the FPS, the EPS is completed and sent to HMRC using the employer's payroll software. Failure to send an EPS may lead to HMRC estimating an amount the employer should pay. A penalty may also arise.

An EPS can be used to notify HMRC in advance if the employer knows that it will pay no employees for a period of up to a year.

 Definition

Employer Payment Summary (EPS) is an electronic report submitted if an employer does not pay any employees in a tax month.

3.2 Content of the EPS

When an EPS is used because no employees were paid, this must include the same employer information as for the FPS, namely:

- Employer PAYE reference

- Accounts Office reference

- the relevant tax year.

Additionally, the employer completes fields which indicate:

- no payments were made to employees in the period

- the start and end dates of the tax month when no employees were paid

- the dates of a period ahead – a minimum of one tax month and a maximum of 12 tax months – when the employer will not pay any employees.

 Reference material

The reference material provided in the real assessment gives the information that the EPS is filed if no employees were paid in a month, and the deadline for submission in the section 'Types of payroll submission'.

Test your understanding 4

Lucia is registered as an employer with HMRC but did not make any payments to staff in the tax month starting 6 November.

Which report/form(s) should Lucia submit to HMRC by 19 December?

A   FPS only

B   EPS only

C   FPS and EPS

D   P45 and EPS

 **4**   **Payments to HMRC**

Chapter 8 explained that an employer deducts PAYE, employee's NICs, and student loan deductions before paying an employee. The employer also suffers employer's NICs, which are added to these deductions.

These amounts are reported on the FPS relating to that payday, as covered earlier in this chapter.

The employer must then pay these amounts to HMRC. If paid by cheque, this must be received by HMRC no later than the 19th of the following month. For example, if an employer paid staff on 30 April, then the deductions are to be paid to HMRC by 19 May. However, funds received electronically do not have to clear until the 22nd of the month.

 Example

Rocki Ltd pays its employees on 30 June. If the company makes payment of PAYE and NICs to HMRC by online banking (i.e. electronically), this must be received by 22 July. Otherwise a payment by cheque must clear by 19 July.

Payments to HMRC may be made on a quarterly, rather than monthly, basis, if the total amount payable is less than £1,500 per month on average. The quarterly payment dates for a tax year are then 19 or 22 July, October, January and April.

Reference material

The reference material provided in the real assessment gives the information about the payment dates in the section on 'Payroll deadlines'. This includes the condition for quarterly payments to be made, and the fact that the month end date for PAYE (i.e. a tax month) is 5th of the month.

Why not look up the correct part of the reference material in the introduction to this text book now? Note that the reference material does not specifically mention payments 'to HMRC'.

Try not to confuse the dates for filing the FPS (on or before the payday) with these dates for making payments of the PAYE and NICs to HMRC.

5 Year-end reporting

5.1 Year-end procedures

At the end of the tax year, the employer must submit the final FPS or EPS, making clear that this is the final report. However, after the end of the tax year, there are further annual forms which must be completed by the employer.

The employer may also be required to make further payments to HMRC in respect of PAYE and different classes of NIC which are not paid over to HMRC during the tax year.

5.2 P60

The employer must complete a form P60 to give to each employee who is employed at the end of the tax year.

This form gives the employee a record of what pay has been earned for the year and the PAYE deductions made.

Specifically, details included on the P60 are:

- the employee's name, NINO, and final tax code

- the employer's name, address and Employer PAYE reference

- the taxable pay of the employee for the tax year, from this employment and any previous employment

- the income tax deducted

- the NICs and student loan deductions for this employment.

The employer's payroll software is usually used to generate the P60s for employees. The employer must give the completed P60 to the employee by 31 May following the end of the tax year.

 Definition

P60 is a form given by an employer to an employee following a tax year, showing the employee's pay for the tax year and the deductions made such as PAYE and NICs.

Below you can find an example of what a P60 looks like:

P60 End of Year Certificate

Tax year to 5 April **2025**

To the employee:

Please keep this certificate in a safe place as you will need it if you have to fill in a tax return. You also need it to make a claim for tax credits and Universal Credit or to renew your claim.

It also helps you check that your employer is using the correct National Insurance number and deducting the right rate of National Insurance contributions.

By law you are required to tell HM Revenue and Customs about any income that is not fully taxed, even if you are not sent a tax return.

HM Revenue and Customs

The figures marked ★ should be used for your tax return, if you get one

Employee's details

Surname

Forenames or initials

National Insurance number

Works/payroll number

Pay and Income Tax details

	Pay	Tax deducted
	£ p	£ p
In previous employments		
		if refund mark 'R'
In this employment	★	
Total for year		
Final tax code		

National Insurance contributions in this employment

NIC table letter	Earnings at the Lower Earnings Limit (LEL) (where earnings are equal to or exceed the LEL)	Earnings above the LEL, up to and including the Primary Threshold (PT)	Earnings above the PT, up to and including the Upper Earnings Limit (UEL)	Employee's contributions due on all earnings above the PT
	£	£	£	£ p

Statutory payments included in the pay 'In this employment' figure above

	£ p		£ p		£ p
Statutory Maternity Pay		Statutory Paternity Pay		Statutory Shared Parental Pay	
Statutory Adoption Pay		Statutory Parental Bereavement Pay			

Other details

Student Loan deductions in this employment (whole £s only) £

Postgraduate Loan deductions in this employment (whole £s only) £

To employee

Your employer's full name and address (including postcode)

Employer PAYE reference

Certificate by Employer/Paying Office
This form shows your total pay for Income Tax purposes in this employment for the year.
Any overtime, bonus, commission etc, Statutory Sick Pay, Statutory Maternity Pay, Statutory Paternity Pay, Statutory Shared Parental Pay, Statutory Parental Bereavement Pay or Statutory Adoption Pay is included.

P60(Single sheet)(2024 to 2025)   **Do not destroy**   HMRC 12/23

Reference material

The reference material provided in the real assessment states that the P60 must be provided to employees, and by what date. It is included in the section on 'Payroll deadlines'.

Why not look up the correct part of the reference material in the introduction to this text book now?

5.3   P11D

The employer must complete another form, a P11D, for each employee who has received taxable expenses or benefits during the tax year.

These are benefits which do not take the form of cash given to the employee. They might include the private use of an asset such as a company car, or the payment by the employer of an expense for the employee, such as private medical insurance. There are some benefits which are exempt, but otherwise employees pay income tax on the benefits they receive from their employer.

The employee does not usually pay NICs on benefits which are reported on the form P11D.

The P11D for an employee will show the employer's name and Employer PAYE reference, along with employee details such as name, NINO and date of birth.

Details are included for specific benefits and expenses such as:

- assets transferred to the employee

- payments made on behalf of the employee

- cars and other assets provided for private use by the employee

- provision of loans from the employer.

The details include the taxable amounts for these benefits and any amounts chargeable to Class 1A NICs, which are discussed further in section 5.4.

The employer must give a copy of the completed P11D form to the employee by 6 July following the end of the tax year. Unlike the form P60, the employer must also submit this to HMRC by the same date.

Definition

P11D is a form given by an employer both to an employee and to HMRC following a tax year, recording the expenses and benefits provided to the employee during the tax year.

 Test your understanding 5

Indicate whether the following statements relate to form P60 or form P11D.

Tick one box on each line.

		P60	P11D
1	Submitted to employees and HMRC.		
2	Provided to employees by 6 July following the end of the tax year.		
3	Records taxable pay for a tax year.		
4	Records taxable benefits for a tax year.		
5	Provided to all employees.		

5.4 P11D(b) and Class 1A NIC

While an employee does not usually pay NICs on P11D benefits, the employer does have to pay NICs on many benefits shown on the P11D. This is known as Class 1A NIC.

The employer must complete a single form P11D(b) to report this Class 1A NIC to HMRC. The P11D(b) form must be submitted by the same date as the P11Ds for all employees i.e. by 6 July following the end of the tax year.

The Class 1A NIC must be paid by 22 July if payment is made electronically (otherwise by 19 July) following the end of the tax year.

Definition

Class 1A NIC is the type of national insurance contributions payable by employers on many taxable benefits which appear on the form P11D.

P11D(b) is a form which an employer must submit to HMRC following a tax year, showing the Class 1A NIC payable for benefits provided in that tax year.

 Reference material

The reference material provided in the real assessment gives the 'Filing deadline for expenses & benefits forms' in the section on 'Payroll deadlines'. The reference material does not specifically use the terms P11D or P11D(b) so you must know where to look for this date.

Why not look up the correct part of the reference material in the introduction to this text book now?

A penalty may arise if the Class 1A NIC is not paid within 30 days of the due date. The penalty is 5% of the unpaid amount if the payment is 30 days late, a further 5% if six months late, and a further 5% if 12 months late.

Reference material

The reference material provided in the real assessment gives the penalty for late payment of Class 1A NICs at the bottom of the section 'Penalties for late payroll payment'. However, the reference material does not specifically mention Class 1A. Instead it refers to 'late payments of amounts due annually or occasionally', so you must know where to look for this penalty.

Why not look up the correct part of the reference material in the introduction to this text book now?

5.5   PAYE Settlement Agreement and Class 1B NIC

Some benefits provided to employees are minor or irregular. In other cases, if a benefit is provided to several employees together, such as a staff party, it may be impracticable to work out the PAYE deductions for individual employees.

In these cases, it may be possible for the employer to enter into a PAYE Settlement Agreement (PSA) with HMRC. This must be approved by HMRC. The employer, rather than the employee, then suffers the cost of the income tax (PAYE).

Such a benefit is not reported on either the employee's P60 or P11D.

The employer (but not the employee) has a national insurance liability, Class 1B.

The deadline for submitting the calculations relating to the PSA of a tax year is 31 July after the tax year.

The deadline for payment of both the PAYE and Class 1B NIC is 22 October (if paying electronically or 19 October otherwise) following the end of the tax year.

 Definition

PAYE Settlement Agreement (PSA) is an approved arrangement between the employer and HMRC that the employer suffers the employee's income tax on a benefit which is minor, irregular, or where it would be impracticable to work out an employee's PAYE deductions.

Class 1B NIC is the type of national insurance contributions payable by employers who have a PSA with HMRC in respect of certain benefits.

The same late payment penalties apply to Class 1B NIC as Class 1A NIC. There is a penalty of 5% of the unpaid amount if 30 days late, a further 5% if six months late, and a further 5% again if 12 months late.

 Reference material

Remember that the penalty for late payment (as for late payment of Class 1A NIC) is given in the section 'Penalties for late payroll payment' under the heading 'Late payments of amounts due annually or occasionally'. Class 1B NIC is not mentioned specifically, so you must know where to look for this penalty.

Why not look up the correct part of the reference material in the introduction to this text book now?

> **Test your understanding 6**
>
> State the due date in each case if the payments are made electronically.
>
> | | | Due date |
> |---|---|---|
> | 1 | Class 1A NICs on taxable benefits provided to employees in the tax year 2024/25. | |
> | 2 | Class 1B NICs for benefits provided to employees in the tax year 2024/25 under a PSA. | |
> | 3 | Class 1 NICs on salary payments made on 30 November 2024. | |

6 Penalties

6.1 Types of penalty

There are two situations where the employer can incur penalties for being late: the late submission of an FPS and the late payment of the PAYE, NICs and student loan deductions.

The employer may also incur a penalty for inaccurate payroll filings.

6.2 Late submissions of payroll filings to HMRC

The employer must submit the FPS on or before the date employees are paid. If the FPS is submitted late, or the expected number of FPSs is not submitted, a late filing penalty is charged. The penalty may also be charged if the employer has not sent an EPS to inform HMRC that no employees have been paid in a tax period.

There are exceptions where the penalties do not apply:

- for the first late submission of the tax year

- the first FPS of a new employer, submitted late but within 30 days of paying an employee – this is not a counted as a late filing when considering the exception above

- usually, where the FPS is filed within three days of the due date, provided this is not persistent behaviour.

The penalty charged depends on the number of employees, and on how late the submission is i.e. two times the monthly penalty is charged if the submission is more than one but less than two months late.

Number of employees	Monthly penalty
1 to 9	£100
10 to 49	£200
50 to 249	£300
250 or more	£400

 Reference material

The reference material provided in the assessment gives the monthly penalties for different numbers of employees when a payroll filing is submitted late. This is included in the section on 'Penalties for late submission of payroll filings'. The section also includes some details of when the penalties may and may not apply.

Why not look up the correct part of the reference material in the introduction to this text book now?

HMRC may send an online non-filing notice if an FPS appears to be missing or a late filing notice if an FPS is late. Such messages warn of penalties and advise how to avoid them.

If an FPS is missing or submitted late and an EPS is not submitted, HMRC may estimate an amount it thinks is due. Submitting the missing FPS or EPS will replace the estimated charge.

6.3 Late payroll payments to HMRC

An employer must pay the PAYE, NICs and student loan deductions to HMRC by the due date, (Section 4). If the payment is late, or if the payment made is less than the amount due, penalties and interest may be charged.

The first late payment in a tax year is not counted as a default but any further late payments are defaults on which a penalty is charged.

The penalty is a percentage of the amount that is paid late and increases with the number of defaults in the tax year. So, for example, for up to three defaults the percentage charged would be 1% of the late payment in each case. A fourth default would be charged at 2% and so on, as shown in the table.

Number of defaults in a tax year	Penalty percentage of late amount
1 to 3	1%
4 to 6	2%
7 to 9	3%
10 or more	4%

Further penalties arise if the payments remain outstanding for more than six months. These penalties apply even for the first late payment, which does not otherwise count as a default.

Period payment is outstanding	Penalty
More than six months	5% of unpaid tax
More than 12 months	A further 5% of unpaid tax

An employer who pays quarterly has only four payment dates in a tax year, and so only the 1% penalty is relevant initially, but the further penalties for payments overdue by more than six months may still apply.

Both late payment and late filing penalties may be avoided if the employer has a 'reasonable excuse'. Such excuses are limited and do not include having insufficient funds to pay.

 Reference material

The reference material provided in the real assessment gives the penalty percentages, depending on the number of defaults in the year, when monthly or quarterly payments are late. These are included in the section on 'Penalties for late payroll payment'. The section also gives the additional penalties for very late payments.

Why not look up the correct part of the reference material in the introduction to this text book now?

Try not to confuse the penalties for late submissions and late payments – use the reference material to help you.

Example

Bricke Ltd was late paying its PAYE and NICs to HMRC for each of September, October, November and December. Each payment was made a few days after the due date except for December's payment which was made eight months late.

The late payment for September does not count as a default and no penalty is charged. Bricke Ltd is charged a penalty of 1% of the amount paid late for each of October, November and December's payments. A further penalty is charged of 5% of the late paid amount for December, as this was paid more than six months late.

Interest is charged daily on all late payments from the due date to the date the payment is made in full.

Similar to late filing, if HMRC thinks a payment is late, it may send an employer a late payment notice through HMRC's PAYE Online service. HMRC sends such messages to encourage payment now and in the future. By sending such reminders, it aims to help employers avoid future penalties.

 Test your understanding 7

Jessie is a sole trader with three employees. She submits the FPS late for both May and June by one week and makes all 12 payments for the tax year late by two weeks.

1   What is the total penalty for late submission in the tax year?

    A   £100

    B   £200

    C   £300

    D   £600

2   What is the percentage penalty applied to the 12th late payment?

    A   4%

    B   5%

    C   10%

    D   14%

7 Communicating payroll information

7.1 Providing information for payroll

Careful operation of payroll is needed so that employees are paid the correct amounts, after all deductions. It is also required for the employer to comply with the tax legislation in relation to both reporting and payment, and so to avoid penalties from HMRC.

Therefore, good communication is needed within the organisation to collect the correct information and to make the payments. This is especially so given the real time nature of reporting.

Payroll payments – to employees and HMRC – represent large cash outflows for a business. The employer must have sufficient funds to pay. The person or department responsible for payroll should communicate when payments will have to be made to those responsible for cash management and budgeting. They may also warn about penalties and interest for failure to pay on time.

 Example

Saj prepares the payroll for a small business.

The owner, Lisa, is concerned about cash flow in the month of January. She suggests delaying by one week the electronic payment to HMRC in respect of December's payroll. The business has made one late payment already in this tax year. Lisa wants to know the consequences if another payment is late.

Saj sends the following email to Lisa.

To: Lisa
From: Saj
Subject: HMRC payroll payments

The payment to HMRC in respect of December's payroll must be made by 22 January.

If the payment is late, interest and penalties may be charged.

One late payment can be made in the tax year without a penalty arising, but another late payment will give rise to a penalty of 1% of the amount that is late.

Saj

Given the amounts of money involved and the consequences if mistakes are made, it is worthwhile a manager reviewing the work of the person preparing the payroll. Several people may be involved in a large organisation. It is important to seek authorisation from a higher level within the organisation, to make payments and submit payroll information to HMRC.

 Example

Richard works in the finance department of a company. He has entered payroll information into the payroll software prior to the August payday.

He notifies the financial controller who authorises the payments to staff and the submission of the FPS to HMRC.

7.2 Sources of information on payroll

Tax rules regarding payroll are extensive. Rates, allowances and limits often change from one tax year to the next, following the government's Budget and related Finance Act.

Payroll software prepares most of the calculations and must be kept up to date for legislative changes. However, it is important for those who operate payroll to keep up with changes, not least to avoid missing deadlines and incurring penalties.

The GOV.UK website is a source of extensive information on payroll matters. It has step by step guides to employing people and running payroll. HMRC produces a regular HMRC Employment Bulletin available online which contains information about changes to the rules. Someone operating payroll can subscribe for PAYE updates from HMRC.

HMRC can be approached for help using an online forum or employer helplines.

Once the payroll department is aware of changes in the rules, these may have to be communicated to other departments. For example, the HR department may be told about a change relating to the required level of pension contributions. This may then be reflected in employment contracts or staff handbooks, or considered when determining new starter pay packages.

Tax legislation is complex. It is likely that someone working in payroll will be asked questions by an employee, or be presented with a scenario relating to payroll which has not dealt with before. Payroll workers should refer queries which are beyond their current experience or expertise to their line manager.

7.3 HMRC powers

HMRC has the power to visit an employer's business premises and inspect records as part of an Employer Compliance Review. The purpose of such a review is to check whether the employer is correctly operating PAYE.

The review may be prompted by errors in the employer's operation of payroll or the employer may be chosen at random.

HMRC will usually notify the employer in advance of the visit. During the visit, the employer must give the HMRC officer access to the payroll records.

If the inspection uncovers errors or inaccuracies on payroll filings, additional PAYE and NICs may become payable, along with interest. A penalty may also arise. The penalty charged is a percentage of the potential lost revenue (PLR) to HMRC. The PLR is the amount of PAYE and/or NICs that should have been paid but were not, because of the error. The percentages applied are the same as those for inaccuracies in a VAT return.

Type of behaviour	Unprompted disclosure %	Prompted disclosure %
Careless	0–30	15–30
Deliberate	20–70	35–70
Deliberate and concealed	30–100	50–100

The penalty can be reduced if the employer discloses the error to HMRC, before HMRC discovers it. This may happen when the employer is preparing for a visit from HMRC, and this would then be a prompted disclosure.

The penalties may arise if the inaccuracy is discovered at any time, regardless of whether a PAYE inspection is due or taking place. The reduction in penalty is greatest if an employer discloses an error without being notified of an Employer Compliance Review. This would be an unprompted, rather than prompted, disclosure.

KAPLAN PUBLISHING

Reference material

The reference material provide in the real assessment gives the percentages for these penalties in the section 'Penalties for inaccuracies in payroll filings'. Therefore, you do not need to learn them but you should understand how the type of behaviour and disclosure affects them.

Why not look up the correct part of the reference material in the introduction to this text book now?

 Test your understanding 8

HMRC intends to visit the offices of Stone Ltd as part of an Employer Compliance Review.

1   What is a possible reason for the review?

    A   All employers are visited annually.

    B   Stone Ltd has asked HMRC to check its records.

    C   Stone Ltd was chosen randomly.

    D   The review is needed for Stone Ltd to register as an employer.

2   What is the maximum penalty for a deliberate and concealed inaccuracy in a payroll filing, if it is discovered by HMRC during the review?

    A   30%

    B   50%

    C   70%

    D   100%

3   Which of the following actions would reduce the possible penalty due to an inaccuracy on a payroll filing submitted by Stone Ltd?

    A   Stone Ltd conceals the inaccuracy by creating a false record.

    B   Stone Ltd notices the inaccuracy and the payroll assistant is warned not to make the same mistake again.

    C   Stone Ltd reveals the inaccuracy during the visit from HMRC.

    D   HMRC discovers the inaccuracy during the visit to Stone Ltd.

7.4 Data protection

An employer's payroll software will hold and use personal data on employees.

As such, the employer must comply with data protection laws including the Data Protection Act 2018 and the UK General Data Protection Regulation (UK GDPR).

 Definition

The Data Protection Act (2018) and the UK General Data Protection Regulation (UK GDPR) are the laws concerning how personal data is held and used, including by employers.

Personal data includes names, contact details and payment information. An employer may also hold sensitive personal data which needs an even greater level of protection. An example may be the fact an employee is a member of a trade union.

The principles of data protection laws, as applied to personal data used in the operation of payroll, are listed here.

- Lawfulness, fairness and transparency
  Data should be used in a way which complies with law, which staff expect, and which they have been told about.

- Purpose limitation
  Data should only be used for the reasons collected, i.e. for the employees to be paid and the correct deductions to be paid.

- Data minimisation
  The employer must collect only the data needed.

- Accuracy
  Personal details must be accurate and kept up to date.

- Storage limitation
  Data should be kept only for as long as needed before being securely destroyed, taking account of the rule for the retention of payroll records covered earlier in this chapter.

- Integrity and security (confidentiality)
  Data must be held securely.

- Accountability
  The employer takes responsibility for compliance with the other principles and keeps records to show this.

Test your understanding 9

Boulder Ltd has breached data protection principles in its operation of payroll. Which principle is breached in each case?

1   An employee Sandra informed the company about her change of address but her emailed payslip shows the old address.

    A   Lawfulness, fairness and transparency

    B   Purpose limitation

    C   Data minimisation

    D   Accuracy

2   The payroll assistant is busy and cannot complete all her work during the working day. She emails employee details to her private email address to complete work on her computer at home.

    A   Data minimisation

    B   Accuracy

    C   Storage limitation

    D   Integrity and security

Test your understanding 10

Indicate whether the following statements about payroll records and software are true or false.

Tick one box on each line.

		True	False
1	Payroll records must be kept for an employee only whilst he or she is employed by the business.		
2	Employers with fewer than ten employees can use HMRC's free payroll software, Basic PAYE Tools.		
3	HMRC has the right to visit an employer's premises and inspect the payroll records.		
4	The penalty for inaccuracies in a payroll filing is £3,000.		
5	A payslip emailed to the wrong employee is an example of a breach of data protection rules.		

Test your understanding answers

Test your understanding 1

1   False – the FPS gives details of starters and leavers in the pay period, but not how long the employees have worked for the employer.

2   False – the employee is given a payslip for each payday, not an FPS. The FPS is submitted to HMRC on or before each payday.

3   True – the FPS shows, amongst other things, each employee's pay and deductions for a pay period.

Test your understanding 2

1   False – Parts 1A, 2 and 3 of the form P45 are given by the former employer to the leaving employee.

2   True – the P45 includes the employee's name, address and NINO.

3   True – the former employer notifies HMRC of the employee's leaving date on the FPS.

Test your understanding 3

1   The correct answer is A.

The FPS must be submitted on or before the date the employees are paid.

2   The correct answer is A.

The P45 does not confirm whether an individual has the right to work in the UK. It provides details necessary for the new employer to make the correct deductions from an employee's pay.

3   The correct answer is C.

The P45 is only issued to an employee on leaving employment and is not a record which is continually updated.

 Test your understanding 4

The correct answer is B.
An EPS is used if the employer paid no employees in the month. An FPS is used to report payments to HMRC. The form P45 is issued by an employer to a leaving employee.

 Test your understanding 5

1   P11D – a P11D is submitted to relevant employees and HMRC. P60s are only given to employees, not submitted to HMRC.

2   P11D – the due date for the P11D is 6 July after the tax year. The due date for the P60 is 31 May after the tax year.

3   P60 – the P60 gives the pay for the year and also the tax and NICs deducted.

4   P11D – an employee with taxable benefits receives a P11D which records these, but also a P60 showing pay and tax deductions.

5   P60 – a P60 is given to all employees but only employees who have received taxable benefits in the tax year are given a form P11D.

Test your understanding 6

1   22 July 2025.

2   22 October 2025.

3   22 December 2024.

 Test your understanding 7

1   The correct answer is A.

The late FPS in May is the first late FPS in the year and does not give rise to a penalty. The employer has three employees and the submission is up to one month late, so the penalty for the late FPS for June is £100.

2   The correct answer is A.

The final late payment is the 11th default in the tax year and so the penalty percentage is 4%. The payment is not at least six months late and so no further late payment penalties arise.

 Test your understanding 8

1   The correct answer is C.

HMRC may choose any employer for an Employer Compliance Review.

2   The correct answer is D.

A deliberate and concealed error may lead to a penalty of 100% of the potential lost revenue.

3   The correct answer is C.

Disclosing to HMRC, even during a visit, may reduce the possible penalty as this would be a prompted disclosure.

Test your understanding 9

1 The correct answer is D.

  Personal data must be accurate and kept up to date.

2 The correct answer is D.

  Personal data must be held securely – sending this to a personal email address and using a home computer is a breach of this principle.

 Test your understanding 10

1 False – for tax purposes, payroll records must be kept for three years from the end of the tax year to which they relate. Additionally, an employer must also consider data protection rules regarding how long data should be stored.

2 True – employers with fewer than ten employees can also use any free or paid-for payroll software by commercial suppliers listed as recognised on the GOV.UK website.

3 True – to check whether an employer is correctly operating PAYE, HMRC is entitled to visit the employer's premises and inspect the payroll records. This is known as an Employer Compliance Review.

4 False – the penalty for an inaccurate payroll filing is a percentage of the potential lost revenue. The penalty for failing to keep records is £3,000.

5 True – emailing a payslip to the wrong employee would breach the principle of integrity and security.

MOCK ASSESSMENT

1 Mock assessment questions

This assessment has 8 tasks.

You should therefore attempt and aim to complete EVERY task.

Each task is independent. You will not need to refer to your answers to previous tasks.

Read every task carefully to make sure you understand what is required.

Where the date is relevant, it is given in the task data.

Both minus signs and brackets can be used to indicate negative numbers unless task instructions state otherwise.

You must use a full stop to indicate a decimal point. For example, write 100.57 NOT 100,57 or 10057.

You may use a comma to indicate a number in the thousands but you don't have to. For example, both 10000 and 10,000 are acceptable.

Task 1 (9 marks)

This task is about understanding and calculating UK tax law principles relating to VAT, registration and deregistration and special schemes.

(a)   Identify whether taxable supplies are being made in each of the following scenarios.   (2 marks)

Statement	Taxable supplies	Not taxable supplies
Sanjeev, who is registered for VAT as a sole trader, collects comics as a hobby. He sells his set of Spiderman comics.		
Bhaskar Ltd, a VAT registered company, sells some children's clothes to Adele. Children's clothes are a zero-rated supply.		

(b) Xander's business, which commenced on 1 February 2024, is currently not registered for VAT.

Monthly turnover consists of

– standard-rated supplies of £12,500

– zero-rated supplies of £8,100

– exempt supplies of £2,900.

From 1 April 2024 his standard-rated supplies increase to £15,400 a month and his exempt supplies to £9,250. His zero-rated supplies remain unchanged.

(i) Complete the following table to show the monthly taxable supplies and the cumulative taxable supplies for the months of February 2024 to July 2024. Enter your answers to the nearest whole pound (£). **(3 marks)**

Statement	Monthly taxable supplies £	Cumulative taxable supplies £
February 2024		
March 2024		
April 2024		
May 2024		
June 2024		
July 2024		

(ii) Identify the date that Xander will need to notify HMRC that his business has exceeded the registration limit. **(1 mark)**

(c) A trader who makes wholly zero-rated supplies can apply to be exempt from registration.

Which of the following options may be a valid reason why the business might prefer NOT to be registered for VAT? **(1 mark)**

A It makes the business's prices cheaper for non-registered customers.

B If the business has a very low level of input VAT.

C Give the appearance of being a bigger and more established business.

(d) Are the following statements true or false?   (2 marks)

Statement	True	False
Vienna Ltd expects its taxable turnover in the next 12 months to be £210,000. Vienna Ltd can join the flat rate scheme.		
Salzburg Ltd is a member of the annual accounting scheme with a VAT year end of March. The company's VAT return must be filed by 7 May of the same year.		

Task 2 (8 marks)

This task is about calculating and accounting for VAT.

(a) Which of the following are required to be shown on a full VAT invoice for a UK supply?   (3 marks)

Tick one box for each line

	Required	Not required
Supplier's name and address		
Customer's name and address		
Customer's registration number		
Method of delivery		
Separate total of any zero-rated goods included in the sale		
Any discount offered		
Delivery note number		

(b) Jake sells goods to Ball Ltd on a sale or return basis. The goods are delivered to Ball Ltd on 4 March. The company has until 30 June in that year to decide whether to keep or return the goods.

Ball Ltd notifies Jake on 10 June that it will keep the goods.

Jake invoices Ball Ltd with an invoice dated 20 June.

What is the tax point date?   (1 mark)

A   4 March

B   10 June

C   20 June

D   30 June

(c)   Aurora has asked you to show her how to calculate VAT at the reduced rate on net and gross amounts.

Complete the table to assist Aurora. Round down your answers to the nearest penny.   **(4 marks)**

Net £	VAT £	Gross £
120.20		
		357.21

Task 3 (12 marks)

This task is about the recovery of input tax.

(a)   **On which of the following purchases of vehicles, bought by registered businesses, can input VAT be reclaimed?   (3 marks)**

Tick one box on each line.

	Reclaim	No reclaim
A car bought for use by Bert, a sole trader. He plans to use the car 60% for his business and 40% privately.		
A car bought by Alana for use solely in her taxi business.		
A car bought by Sheard Ltd for general use as a pool car by all its employees.		
A car bought by Bee Ltd for the sole use of its managing director who uses the car for all his business and private use.		
A van bought by Dennis for use by one of his team leaders.		

(b) A registered business supplies goods that are a mixture of standard-rated and exempt.

Which of the following statements is true? (1 mark)

Select ONE answer.

A   All the input VAT relating to standard-rated goods can be reclaimed but never any relating to exempt supplies

B   None of the input VAT can be reclaimed

C   All of the input VAT can be reclaimed

D   All of the input VAT can be reclaimed providing certain (de minimis) conditions are met

(c) A business that makes only standard-rated supplies wrote off the following bad debts on 31 January 2025.

	Date payment due	Amount (VAT-inclusive) £
Carder Ltd	20 February 2024	543.60
Honey Ltd	15 April 2024	950.42
Tree Ltd	17 November 2024	1,100.00

For each bad debt identified:

(i) **Identify whether or not they are eligible for bad debt relief in the VAT return for the quarter ended 31 March 2025.**

(ii) **Calculate the amount of bad debt relief available. Round down figures to the nearest penny.** (4 marks)

Bad debt	Eligible for bad debt relief	Not eligible for bad debt relief	Amount of bad debt relief available £
Carder Ltd			
Honey Ltd			
Tree Ltd			

(d) Hussnan is a VAT registered sole trader. He uses his car 60% for business purposes. The car has CO_2 emissions of 168g/km. The business has paid for fuel totalling £1,860 (this figure includes VAT) in the quarter ended 30 September 2024.

(i) **Complete the following statement.**

The correct VAT-inclusive fuel scale charge for the quarter to 30 September 2024 is:

A   £403.00

B   £139.00

C   £420.00

D   £134.00

(ii) **Calculate the amount of input tax that Hussnan can reclaim on the fuel in the quarter. Show your answer to the nearest pence.**

£

(3 marks)

(e) Hussnan received an invoice from a supplier for goods of value £850.00 excluding VAT at the standard rate. The supplier offered Hussnan a 5% prompt payment discount if payment was received within ten days.

Hussnan took advantage of the prompt payment discount.

Calculate the amount that Hussnan can recover as input tax. Round down to the nearest penny. **(1 mark)**

£

Task 4 (8 marks)

This task is about preparing, calculating and adjusting information for VAT returns.

(a) Badella Ltd has returned some faulty goods to Lane plc and issued Lane plc with a debit note.

What is the effect on VAT of processing this debit note in the books of Badella Ltd? **(2 marks)**

Select ONE answer.

A   Input tax will increase

B   Input tax will decrease

C   Output tax will increase

D   Output tax will decrease

(b) A business that consistently pays £3,000 of VAT to HMRC each quarter has issued a credit note to a customer for £393 (VAT-inclusive).

What will be the effect of processing this credit note on the VAT liability for this quarter? **(2 marks)**

A   VAT due to HMRC will increase by £65.50

B   VAT due to HMRC will decrease by £65.50

C   VAT due to HMRC will increase by £78.60

D   VAT due to HMRC will decrease by £78.60

(c) Ubersee Ltd, a company resident in the UK, is registered for VAT in the UK.   The company trades internationally and uses postponed accounting for its imports of goods. Yolanda is new at Ubersee Ltd and has asked for your help to understand the VAT implications of trade overseas.

Identify whether the following statements are true or false to help Yolanda. **(2 marks)**

Statement	True	False
Ubersee Ltd buys services from Dienstleistungen Inc, a company in Rwanda. For VAT purposes, the place of supply of these services is the UK.		
When Ubersee Ltd imports goods, it must pay output tax immediately as the goods enter the UK.		

(d) Yolanda has noticed that the bank reconciliation for Ubersee Ltd was not completed for the previous quarter.

She has identified two transactions that need to be posted to the accounting software.

Calculate the changes that need to be made to the figures for output and input tax for each transaction. Round your answers down to the nearest penny. If there is no change enter 0.00.

(2 marks)

Transaction	Output tax £	Input tax £
A direct debit for payment of electricity of £325.50. The supporting documentation shows this includes VAT at 5%.		
Proceeds for sale of a machine for £5,040 (including VAT). Ubersee Ltd had claimed VAT on the original purchase.		

Task 5 (12 marks)

This task is about verifying VAT returns.

(a) Libretto Ltd started to trade on 1 October 2024 using the standard VAT scheme. However, the computer system which produces the VAT returns was incorrectly set up for cash accounting.

The draft VAT return for the first quarter shows the following figures:

	£
Box 1	22,760.56
Box 4	19,870.00

The VAT liability per the VAT control account shows an amount due to HMRC of £4,091.56.

All purchases are made for cash but there was an amount of trade receivables of £7,206 (VAT inclusive) outstanding at the end of the quarter.

Complete the table below to reconcile the figure in the draft VAT return to the figure in the VAT account. Work to the nearest pence **(2 marks)**

	£
Amount due per draft VAT return	
Output VAT on trade receivables	
Amount due per the VAT account	4,091.56

(b) The VAT account of Red Mason Ltd for the quarter ended 31 March 2025 is currently showing:

Output tax of £79,562.68

Input tax of £47,083.21

No adjustments have yet been made for the following:

Fuel scale charges with total VAT of £85.83

Purchase of a van for the business costing £10,690 before VAT

What figures should appear in the VAT return? **(4 marks)**

(i)   Box 1 ………………………….

(ii)   Box 4 ………………………….

(c) Tawny plc has discovered that VAT of £24,000 on a sales invoice of £120,000 (VAT-exclusive) was omitted from the last VAT return by mistake.

No correction has yet been made for this error.

The current quarter's VAT return has a Box 6 figure of £2,750,000.

(i)   Which ONE of the following statements is true?

A   The error is small enough to include on the current VAT return.

B   The error must be separately notified to HMRC.

(ii) Complete the following statement about the error.

The error will (increase/decrease) (input/output) tax.   **(4 marks)**

(d) **Identify whether the following statements regarding the VAT return are true or false. You should assume both traders are VAT registered.** **(2 marks)**

Statement	True	False
Avery buys a car that they will use 20% for non-business purposes. Input tax on this transaction must be added to box 4 of the VAT return.		
Ivy Ltd has received a credit note from a supplier. The VAT will be deducted from box 4 of the VAT return.		

Task 6 (11 marks)

This task is about VAT rules on record keeping, filing and payment/repayment, including non-compliance issues.

(a) Zee Ltd is a VAT-registered business filing quarterly VAT returns. Zee Ltd has always filed its returns on time, but the VAT return for quarter ended 30 June 2024 was not submitted until 2 September 2024 and its VAT liability was paid on the same date.

Identify whether the following statements are true or false.

(3 marks)

Statement	True	False
The VAT return for the quarter ended 30 June 2024 was due to be submitted on 7 August 2024		
The submission of the VAT return for quarter ended 30 June 2024 will lead to one penalty point which, as long as the threshold is not breached, will expire after one year.		
The late payment for the quarter ended 30 June 2024 will lead to a penalty being charged based on 2% of the VAT due.		

(b) White Tail Ltd has a VAT year ended 31 May.

    (i) **Until what date must the company keeps its business records for the period ended 31 May 2024?**

        A   31 May 2025

        B   31 May 2026

        C   31 May 2029

        D   31 May 2030

    (ii) **What is the maximum penalty if White Tail Ltd do not keep their records until this date?**

        £ _____

    (iii) **Which TWO of the following are records that must be retained for VAT purposes?**

        A   Employment contracts

        B   Sales invoices

        C   Bank statements

        D   Business tenders   **(4 marks)**

(c) The owner of Ashy Bars and Restaurants is aware that the business exceeded the VAT registration limit over eight months ago. He has asked his finance department to alter records to hide this fact and has failed to register.

Complete the following statements about Ashy Bars and Restaurants.   **(3 marks)**

The business will be charged a penalty at a maximum of [30%/70%/100%] of [profit for the period/potential lost revenue].

The business [will/will not] have to pay over to HMRC the VAT it should have charged its customers in this period.

(d) Chapman Ltd is a VAT-registered business making a mix of standard and zero-rated supplies.

On 1 June 2024, it starts making exempt supplies and reduces the amount of standard-rated supplies it makes.

Which ONE of the following statements is true?   **(1 mark)**

    A   This change will be reflected when Chapman Ltd prepares the next VAT return so it does not have to notify HMRC.

    B   This change should be notified to HMRC within 30 days.

Task 7 (12 marks)

This task is about principles of payroll.

(a) **Match the definitions below with the correct term.**

Definition	Option
The amount an employee receives for a period after all deductions	
The amount of pay after any tax free deductions	
The total earnings for the period before deductions	

(3 marks)

Option	
1	Taxable pay
2	Net pay
3	Gross pay

(b) **Identify whether the following statements about registering as an employer are true or false.** (3 marks)

Statement	True	False
In a company where a director is the only employee, registration for PAYE is not required.		
Registration as an employer must be made before the first payday.		
Ethel is a sole trader. She has recently recruited Dale on a part-time basis, paying him £200 a week. She must now register as an employer.		

(c) Gorse Ltd employs Jasmine who works flexible hours each month. Below are the details of Jasmine's pay for October 2024:

	£
120 hours at £13.50 an hour	1,620.00
Income tax	98.40
Employee's national insurance contributions	98.76
Employer's national insurance contributions	122.54
Employee's pension contributions	81.00
Employer's pension contributions	129.60

Complete the table below showing which THREE of the options below HMRC requires to be shown on Jasmine's payslip. Enter the amounts to be included for each to the nearest pence.

Option number	£

Option	
1	Gross pay
2	Net pay
3	Employee's national insurance contributions
4	Employer's national insurance contributions
5	Employee's pension contributions
6	Employer's pension contributions
7	Income tax
8	Total deductions

(6 marks)

Task 8 (8 marks)

This task is about reporting information on VAT and payroll.

(a) You are a junior accountant working for Bluebell Ltd and your responsibilities include preparing and submitting the company's quarterly VAT return.

Identify which TWO of the following events should prompt you to check for updates to the software you use for VAT returns.

(2 marks)

A   When your friend at another firm tells you they are checking theirs.

B   Notification from HMRC about change in the VAT status of goods being sold.

C   On notification from software provider.

D   When you have a quiet period at work.

(b) The VAT return for the quarter ended 31 December 2024 shows the following amounts.

The figure in Box 3 of the return is	£8,478.96
The figure in Box 4 of the return is	£4,999.40
The figure in Box 6 of the return is	£42,395
The figure in Box 7 of the return is	£25,347

The business does not pay by direct debit.

Complete the following statements. **(2 marks)**

The amount in Box 5 of the return is: £ [   ]

The VAT liability must be paid to HMRC by: [/   /   ]

(c) You have identified that Bluebell Ltd may be able to save VAT under the flat rate scheme. The relevant flat rate percentage for Bluebell Ltd is 6.5% and it is not a limited cost business.

(i)   Calculate the amount of VAT due if Bluebell Ltd were registered under the flat rate scheme (ignore the 1% discount). Enter your answer to the nearest penny.

(2 marks)

£ [   ]

(ii) Identify the course of action to take with your findings.

(1 mark)

    A   Do nothing, you don't want to question your manager's decisions

    B   Query with HMRC the calculation of the sector percentage for the flat rate scheme

    C   Discuss with your line manager

(d) You work for Thistle Ltd in the payroll department. John, one of the employees, has asked to see the payslip of Javier, one of the other employees, as he thinks he is being paid less than him.

What is the correct response here?   **(1 mark)**

    A   You can never reveal Javier's payroll information to anyone else.

    B   Agree to reveal the information as long as John does not let Javier know that you have done so.

    C   You can only reveal the information to John with Javier's permission.

2 Mock assessment answers

Task 1

(a)

Statement	Taxable supplies	Not taxable supplies
Sanjeev, who is registered for VAT as a sole trader, collects comics as a hobby. He sells his set of Spiderman comics.		✓
Bhaskar Ltd, a VAT registered company, sells some children's clothes to Adele. Children's clothes are a zero-rated supply.	✓	

Sanjeev is not making a sale in the course of his business, so this is not a taxable supply.

Zero-rated goods are taxable supplies.

(b) (i)

Statement	Monthly taxable supplies £	Cumulative taxable supplies £
February 2024	20,600	20,600
March 2024	20,600	41,200
April 2024	23,500	64,700
May 2024	23,500	88,200
June 2024	23,500	111,700
July 2024	23,500	135,200

(ii) The correct answer is 30 July 2024.

The VAT registration limit is exceeded when the historic test is performed at the end of May. Xander then has 30 days from the end of June to notify HMRC.

(c) The correct answer is B.

As the business makes wholly zero-rated supplies, it would be charging VAT at 0% if it were registered, and could recover any input VAT suffered.

This has no effect on its prices and the amount it charges its customers and therefore A is incorrect.

Small businesses can give the appearance of being bigger and more established if they choose to register for VAT This can be very appealing to customers, lenders, investors, and suppliers because they will assume the company's turnover is in excess of the VAT registration threshold.

However, if the business has a low level of input VAT to recover, it may not want to be registered as the administrative burden and costs may outweigh the benefit of input VAT recovery.

(d)

Statement	True	False
Vienna Ltd expects its taxable turnover in the next 12 months to be £210,000. Vienna Ltd can join the flat rate scheme.		✓
Salzburg Ltd is a member of the annual accounting scheme with a VAT year end of March. The company's VAT return must be filed by 7 May of the same year.		✓

To join the flat rate scheme Vienna must not expect its taxable turnover to exceed £150,000. Once in the scheme, it must leave once its taxable turnover exceeds £230,000.

Salzburg Ltd has two months to file its VAT return after the year end i.e. by 31 May of the relevant year.

Task 2

(a) Full VAT invoice

	Required	Not required
Supplier's name and address	✓	
Customer's name and address	✓	
Customer's registration number		✓
Method of delivery		✓
Separate total of any zero-rated goods included in the sale	✓	
Any discount offered	✓	
Delivery note number		✓

(b) The correct answer is C.

The basic tax point for goods sent out on sale or return is the earlier of:

– the date the goods are accepted (i.e. 10 June), or

– the cut-off date for accepting the goods (provided this is no longer than 1 year after delivery) (i.e. 30 June)

This would make the basic tax point 10 June.

However, as an invoice has been raised within 14 days of the basic tax point, the actual tax point date is moved to the date of the invoice under the 14-day rule.

(c)

Net £	VAT £	Gross £
120.20	6.01	126.21
340.20	17.01	357.21

The reduced rate of VAT is 5%.

To calculate the VAT from the net (VAT exclusive amount) multiply by 5%.

To calculate the VAT from the gross (VAT inclusive amount) multiply by 5/105 or the simplified VAT fraction of 1/21.

Task 3

(a) Input tax reclaim on vehicles

	Reclaim	No reclaim
A car bought for use by Bert, a sole trader. He plans to use the car 60% for his business and 40% privately.		✓
A car bought by Alana for use solely in her taxi business.	✓	
A car bought by Sheard Ltd for general use as a pool car by all its employees.	✓	
A car bought by Bee Ltd for the sole use of its managing director who uses the car for all his business and private use.		✓
A van bought by Dennis for use by one of his site team leaders.	✓	

If a car has any private use at all, none of the input tax can be recovered.

(b) The correct answer is D

If a partially exempt business does not exceed the de minimis limit all of its input tax can be recovered. If the limit is exceeded only the input tax relating to taxable supplies can be recovered.

(c)

Bad debt	Eligible for bad debt relief	Not eligible for bad debt relief	Amount of bad debt relief available £
Carder Ltd	✓		90.60
Honey Ltd	✓		158.40
Tree Ltd		✓	

A debt must be written off and more than six months old before the input tax can be reclaimed.

It is important that you follow task instructions in the exam. If asked to round in a particular way for a task you will only score the marks allocated if you do so.

(d) (i) The correct answer is A.

The correct fuel scale charge can be found by using your reference material. You should always round down CO_2 emissions to the nearest 5g/km to use this table.

The fuel scale is treated as an output. Output tax of £403.00 × 20/120 = £67.17 will be added to Hussnan's VAT return for the quarter.

(ii) The correct answer is £310.00.

By charging himself a scale charge Hussnan can then recover all of the input tax paid on the fuel, with no further adjustments being required for private use.

(e) The correct answer is £161.50.

As Hussnan paid on time to qualify for the discount, the VAT payable will be calculated on the value of the goods after the deduction of this. The VAT charged will be:

£850.00 × 95% × 20% = £161.50.

Task 4

(a) The correct answer is B.

A debit note is issued by a customer and reduces their purchases (inputs). The VAT on this will reduce input tax.

(b) The correct answer is B

A credit note is deducted from output tax meaning it reduces VAT due.

As the amount is VAT-inclusive, it must be multiplied by 20/120 to find the VAT of £65.50 (£393 × 20/120).

(c)

Statement	True	False
Ubersee Ltd buys services from Dienstleistungen Inc, a company in Rwanda. For VAT purposes, the place of supply of these services is the UK.	✓	
When Ubersee Ltd imports goods it must pay output tax immediately as the goods enter the UK.		✓

When a UK business purchases services from an overseas country the place of supply is deemed to be the UK.

Under the postponed VAT accounting scheme output tax on imports of goods is accounted for under the customer's next VAT return.

(d)

Transaction	Output tax £	Input tax £
A direct debit for payment of electricity of £325.50. The supporting documentation shows this includes VAT at 5%.		£15.50
Proceeds for sale of a machine for £5,040 (including VAT). Ubersee Ltd had claimed VAT on the original purchase.	£840.00	

Task 5

(a) **The correct answer is:**

	£
Amount due per draft VAT return	2,890.56
Output VAT on trade receivables	1,201.00
Amount due per the VAT account	4,091.56

Under the cash accounting scheme, the VAT due on receivables is not included in output tax until it is paid. Under the standard scheme it will be included at tax point date (likely to be invoice date).

(b) **(i)** **Box 1 (£79,562.68 + £85.83) = £79,648.51**

The VAT on the fuel scale charge is treated as extra output tax so added to box 1.

(ii) **Box 4 (£47,083.21 + (£10,690 × 20%)) = £49,221.21**

VAT can be reclaimed on the purchase of capital items for the business. The exception to this is cars which have any private use at all.

(c) (i)   The correct answer is A.

Errors between £10,000 and £50,000 can be included on the VAT return provided they are no more than 1% of the Box 6 figure.

In this case, 1% of £2,750,000 is £27,500.

(ii)   The correct statement is:

The error will **increase output** tax.

(d)

Statement	True	False
Avery buys a car that they will use 20% for non-business purposes. Input tax on this transaction must be added to box 4 of the VAT return.		✓
Ivy Ltd has received a credit note from a supplier. The VAT will be deducted from box 4 of the VAT return.	✓	

Avery will not have been able to reclaim any input tax on the purchase of the car as it is not being used 100% for business purposes.

A purchase credit note reduces the value of inputs. The VAT on it is deducted from input tax.

Task 6

(a)

Statement	True	False
The VAT return for the quarter ended 30 June 2024 should have been submitted on 7 August 2024	✓	
The submission of the VAT return for quarter ended 30 June 2024 will lead to one penalty point which, as long as the threshold is not breached, will expire after one year		✓
The late payment for the quarter ended 30 June 2024 will lead to a penalty being charged based on 2% of the VAT due.	✓	

Submission of the VAT return should be within one month and 7 days after the end of the return period.

When a return is submitted late, a penalty point is awarded which will expire after **two** years as long as the threshold has not been breached by then.

Since the tax is paid between 16-30 days late, a penalty of 2% would be charged.

(b) (i)   The correct answer is D.

Business records must be retained for six years.

(ii)   The correct answer is £500.

This can be found in your reference materials.

(iii) The correct answers are B and C.

(c) The correct statements are:

The business will be charged a penalty at a maximum of **100%** of **potential lost revenue**.

The business **will** have to pay over to HMRC the VAT it should have charged its customers in this period.

Ashy Bars and Restaurants have deliberately not disclosed that the registration limit has been exceeded and have taken steps to hide this from HMRC. This would be classed as a deliberate error with concealment. The error is charged at a maximum of 100% of potential lost revenue, this means the VAT that HMRC have lost out on.

(d) The correct answer is B

This information can be found in your reference material.

Task 7

(a) The correct answers are:

Definition	Option
The amount an employee receives for a period after all deductions	2
The amount of pay after any tax free deductions	1
The total earnings for the period before deductions	3

(b)

Statement	True	False
In a company where a director is the only employee, registration for PAYE is not required.		✓
Registration as an employer must be made before the first payday.	✓	
Ethel is a sole trader. She has recently recruited Dale on a part-time basis, paying him £200 a week. She must now register as an employer.	✓	

Registration is required even if there is a single employee as long as that employee earns more than £123 a week. A business must register before the first payday (but no more than two months before starting to pay employees).

(c)

Option number	£
1 Gross pay	1,620.00
2 Net pay	1,341.84
8 Total deductions	278.16

Jasmine will receive her salary after deductions of income tax, employee's national insurance and pension contributions. The employer's contributions are not deductions for Jasmine, but they are an extra cost to her employer Gorse Ltd.

The options do not need to be entered in the same order as the model to score maximum marks on this question.

Task 8

(a) **The correct statements are B and C.**

(b) **The correct answers are:**

The amount in Box 5 of the return is **£3,479.56,** this is the amount due to HMRC.

The VAT liability must be paid to HMRC by **7 February 2025**.

The VAT liability is calculated as Box 3 (output tax) less Box 4 (input tax). As the company does not pay by direct debit it must be paid to HMRC by one month and seven days after the end of the VAT return period.

(c) (i) **The correct answer is:**

The VAT is calculated by multiplying the VAT inclusive turnover for the period by the flat rate percentage.

(£42,395 + £8,478.96) × 6.5% = **£3,306.81**

(ii) **The correct answer is C.**

(d) **The correct answer is C.**

The payroll information is confidential. You should only reveal this with Javier's authority.

INDEX

KAPLAN PUBLISHING